MW00874357

Dedication

I'll first like to dedicate my second book to The Most High, my Heavenly Father, for all he has done for me and His people. I thank God even more for what He has instore for me and my future as I go down this path: only He designed for me. So glory to Him for His many blessings, miracles and sacrifice. I'll also like to dedicate this book to my falling cousins who are now angles along with my friends I lost who are in this book yet won't be here to read what I wrote for them. This includes my cousins Noodie, Lucky, (due to gun violence) #1papa, fav cousin Niesha (who was supposed to go far with me in the book world) and my dear friend Turtle. I had plans for both Niesha and Turtle considering how gifted, talented they were as well as having a heart bigger than mines (my opinion). My goals and God's plans are a little different just know I love all of you all and will finish what I started. Lastly, I dedicate this book to all my survivors out there making ends meet as we go through our trials and tribulations. Keep fighting and move forward; because it is what it is. Remember it's not about what you walk away from but what you walk away with. To all my readers I thank you all for taking the time to read my books as you understand things in my perspectives. Just know I have more books to come and I thank you for your support. For I'm being used by God for His reasons yet for my soul's sake. Amen..........

Walking Testimony

Chapter 1

Fresh outta high school headed straight to college, I felt good and was thrilled I was finally done with my mom and her drama. I assumed all my problems were gone away, little did I know everywhere I went it was a problem sooner than later. From this day forward I wasn't looking back. That night of my 1st day I talked to my roomies as well as the resident assistance (Ra) and after the meeting I went to bed waiting to go to Cleveland for prayer then that Sunday was my ceremony where I receive my purity ring. Leaving the next evening I went to prayer thanks to the member of prayer and afterwards I went over Meka house for the night. The next day I went to church as planned and told everyone about my big event including Meka, papa Toby to my dad and guess what no one showed besides my mom and my #1 papa who both came late and afterwards I waited for one of the church members to take me back to Akron. After getting back in Akron that Sunday night I walked around campus with Britt and went back home where I prepared myself for the 1st day of school. I was glad I stayed in a house then a dorm room where I have to share a bathroom with more than 20 women and since I was still on the shot I wasn't trying to be bothered with the other students on their periods so I was lucky to stay in the house not knowing how much it cost. Waking up that mooring I got dress and headed out to my 1st class of the day which was my writing class listening to Yolanda Adams "Never give up" to "I'm going to be ready" to " I believe" as I walked in my first class taking the look of my students and the classroom. I already assumed that this was going to be my least favorite class little did I know as I was attending this class it will be one of my favorite classes and because of my teacher I decided to write this book. After this class I had over 30 minutes break before my next class which was oral communication class on the opposite side of campus. I had a math2 class plus my American government class and after the last class was over I was exhausted from a long day plus I had homework the first day after receiving my entire syllabus for those four classes. That schedule was like that Monday, Wednesday and Fridays only while Tuesday I had writing and math2 only and on Thursday I had student success seminar which was a three hour class so I made a mental note on which class to go to on which day. That night I was informed of an ice breaker party that I was too drunk to even attend and had a major hangover not attending my two classes the next day. Instead I spent my second day of class sleep in my bed as my other four roommates went in and out the house. By the third day I was back on track taking notes and doing classwork. Since I didn't buy my books yet I had to use my classmates book which is how I met people from Turtle to MzAk47 and more people who chilled with me during breaks. Catching up on work I was cool and by the end of the week I had two pop quizzes and a writing assignment. For the next three weeks I got adjusted to my new schedule and on weekends I spent going to Cleveland chilling with Meka, Keke and Rae. The first weekend we chilled at her house with her brothers including "Kid" Lil mace and J along with her cousin Man and the neighborhood kids. Even though "kid" kissed Rae in was supposed to be in a relationship with Rae I started to develop feelings for him ever since the kiss on the stairs and us chilling from time to time yet no one knew but me. On the second weekend we visited Meka co-workers going to a mini mansion somewhere in Shaker Heights having a house full of people playing beer pong, drinking, smoking and dancing and everything was going fine. Long story short after I was geeked to the max I ended up in the bathroom on the 1st floor with this guy Dre giving him a quickie before returning to the party. Not really paying attention to what I was doing nor was it in my mind that I just completed a class about not having sex which led me to be shocked as fuck at what I just did so I grabbed Meka and told her what happen. I was pissed that I just took a class about being non sexual and since I only had sex five times throughout my whole high school year that I felt bad for doing it and needed someone to vent to yet our conversation was over with as soon as a crowd came in the bathroom while others stood outside the restroom. Six girls and two boys were in the restroom including Meka and I; then the lights were off and we were in the dark for a while. I can't say what others did since it was dark but can tell you that another guy attempted to stick his dick in me from behind, sliding his dick thru my red thong underneath my white dress which is the same white dress I wore to my ceremony at church.

Afterwards everyone was leaving the bathroom one by one yet when it was my turn I was stopped by a girl and the same guy who tried to fuck me saying "I'm not leaving out of here". Scared a little I called for Meka yet Rae showed up saving the day and I left her in the bathroom with the girl I knew now was gay. I continue to party till we all past out in different beds on different floors waking up the next day going back to San's house with Meka. Since it was now Sunday I knew I had to leave later that night to go back to Akron so I chilled over Meka house. Over there I let Rae redo my hair same time Man let me in on the info about "Kid" fucking with Man cousin and word on the street they were a couple and after doing a little investigation of my own I realized I wasn't the only girl yet I should of seen that coming knowing he was fucking with Rae first yet still no one knew I had a thing for him but since I had this info I figured fuck it just like he's doing the females I'll treat him as well as the next as option. Even though I never cared for a nigga he was the second one who I felt was misleading me and I wasn't having that fighting over a nigga with another bitch so I decide to keep it at a friendly level nothing more and it could be less yet I wasn't letting "Kid" know what I knew. The third weekend I stayed at home doing homework and since I now had my school books the copying answers off someone else was dead so I did my work by myself and having test in each class but my student success seminar. I also had to drop my American Government class and change my meal plan after taking out a loan to pay for my semester thanks to my mom doing my financial aid two months prior which only let me get 5,500$ for school and since my housing was over three thousand plus a meal plan I was in debt faster than I could blink. After the 4th week I got hipped to a group of girls three to be exact didn't like me or the group I chilled with and I don't know why yet I didn't pay them no mind. College life was turning out good from parting at the clubs to school and I fell in love with it all. Just as there were good things so were the bad. For starters I slowly was falling out with my roommates one by one. We went from shopping together to partying together yet all good things come to an end in this lifetime. Starting with Kate who was the only white girl in the house. I never had a big major problem yet I simply didn't like her because of her color and I assumed she felt the same little did I know her and her boyfriend didn't look at me how I look at them and after having a convo with Trooty about Kate miss white girl came in my room and before she could make out one word she said I hopped out my bed ready to fight thinking we were going to fight. Instead she told me about myself and how she love black people including her bestie who was black as well and after that I felt bad for not giving her a chance yet she wasn't as off the hook. I peeped how she will leave the bathroom dirty having hair pieces everywhere to keeping the kitchen dirty after cooking for her and her boyfriend. Her room was also dirty but since I didn't share a room with her I wasn't tripping about that yet Britt-britt was. The 2nd person I develop beef for was my roomie Kandi who knew my cousin Missty since they both went to the same high school. What started the house vs Kandi was the fact that she was a nasty person to live with. I peeped as three out of five girls kept the house clean which was Britt, Trooty and I while Kandi only washed her clothes while Kate barely was there and when she was she only kept herself clean. Kandi or Kate never took turns cleaning the kitchen or bathroom and didn't even take out the trash and slowly but surely I was getting pissed the fuck off. What was nasty to me was when the time of the month came around she will leave her pads in the bathroom garbage can wrapped in tissue with no trash bag yet what made me mad was she will wait till one of the girls in the house will have to tell her to take the trash out as if we was find smelling fish. Since I was taking out the trash a lot I decide after I cleaned the kitchen garbage can for the I don't know how many times I did it and hid it in the basement under the stairs and let the house know that everybody is responsible for taking their on trash out from here on out. After the trash incident everyone was doing their own thing but one thing me, Trooty and Britt do was hit the clubs. Everything was going by managing the changes in all of our friendship yet Kandi slow started to piss me the fuck off. For starters Kandi took it upon herself to eat the "C" part of my crunch bar without asking me and after Trooty informed me about it, I went off, having my other roommates calm me down I decide to let it go on the strength I was about to go to the sky lounge that night. As I continue getting dress using the mirror in the coolest Kandi was using, Kandi cousin on the other hand decide to be petty and tell Kandi I was in the closet and just as she was informed she had the nerve to ask me to get out her closet and to not use her mirror as if this closet wasn't the property of the school. Ignoring her I finished getting dress and left meeting some of my classmates at the club along with Trooty being there. After a night of partying that Thursday night I went home to prepare myself for my three classes that Friday plus it was my mom b-day and I had a surprise ice cream cake for her. Waking up I prepared myself for school that day yet just as I was grabbing my usual blue mountain dew drink plus my pop tart I heard Kandi voice as I past the stairs. Being nosey I listened in on the convocation realizing she was talking shit about me. What pissed me off is she waited till she thought I was gone to talk shit about me. What triggered me was when she was talking about me dancing with a guy saying "I can't believe she was dancing with that musty guy (talking about one of the guys I danced with) with her broke dirty ass". As soon as those words came out I dropped my stuff running upstairs catching both my roommates off guard. Not saying a word I went in my desk and pulled out a handful of panties and threw it at Kandi not caring it hit Trooty follow by some change on my desk saying "where am I broke or dirty at?" Trooty then jumped out her bed separating us to as hateful words were exchanged waking up my other two roommates yet that didn't stop me from talking shit. Not caring how late I was going to be, I continued arguing with Kandi following her till she went downstairs so I spit on her barely missing her draw string ponytail and after she left I did the same headed to my writing glass yet when I got there class was being dismissed early after being in there for 15minutes so I was pissed off even more. Since I had free time before my oral communication class I decide to pick up my mom cake yet when I got there, Baskin Robins pissed me off by fucking up my order. Instead of a blue rose cake saying happy 38th b-day mommy it was a kid flower so I was angry even more for the third time and I took the cake home and set it in the fridge and off to my second class I went. It was clear to everyone that I was pissed yet I didn't let that stop me from doing my work. After I was done with school for the day I rush home to go pack and was waiting on my papa Toby to pick me up meanwhile I went on my laptop where I was listing to music on Pandora and doing some of my homework. As I decide to take a break I went on Facebook to see what was in my newsfeed when I came across a video that was posted by Trooty. As I watched the video I noticed it was from the argument the night before staring Kandi and I and after I seen Kandi comment on there I did the same going back and forth with her threating her that I will post a pic of her with one of her dirty panties and post it on Facebook. After I said what I said, I logged off and started to have a convo with my mom letting her know that I was coming to Cleveland that night. Just as I was conversation out of nowhere I was punched on the right side of my jaw causing me to drop my phone disturbing the talk I was having with my mom. Just as fast as that happened I jumped up attacking Kandi punching her with my one hand repeating my fist to her face fighting from my room to the hallway and down the stairs. The fight stopped as Kandi fell down the stairs damn near and the shit talking began and I was right at her neck telling her to wipe the blood off her face and come up here and fight me and she did as she was told meeting my fist on the way up the stairs and the fighting began from the steps to the hallway passing the bathroom and we both was putting and work yet I was doing more till my right ankle rolled and since I can't move my foot I fell causing Kandi to have the upper hand hitting me as she was over me yet I was still hitting back. It didn't take long for Britt and her best friend along with Trooty best friend to separate us two leaving me in the hallway while everybody but Kandi cousin was in my room with the door locked. Of Corse I still wanted to fight for I wasn't done releasing build up anger I had inside me over the years from what my mom put me through to the kids at high school inside. As they wouldn't let me in my room I heard my phone go off and since I got customize ringtones for certain people I knew my mom and "Kid" was calling me and because they wouldn't let me in all I did was get even more angry. As I attempted to break in the door by using a knife it was a failure so the only thing I could think of was break down the door and using my body a bitch broke that door and as soon as it opened up everyone ran out the room but Kandi who was behind the door and as soon as I seen her the fight began again from the room to the hallway till I was getting tired and chased her out the house damn near throwing her Nike tennis shoes in the dumpster. As I watched as Kandi followed her cousin to the Grant building I called a fellow classmate Des who was in that SIG bus and going with her we went inside the Grant building as I was letting her in on the fight that just took place. After a while I lost track of time and realized my papa Toby was supposed to pick me up 30minutes ago and after talking to him to remind him to pick me up I waited for him as I went back home where I informed both my mom and "Kid" about the fight and before I could finish my convo with "Kid" telling him about the fight I was told by my roommate that the Ra wanted to speak to me. Speaking to the staff I was told that I was to report to Judicial Affairs in the student union building. Since papa Toby was now waiting on me, I cut the meeting short and was told that Kandi will be moving out by the time I was to get back. Going back to Cleveland that night I spent the remainder day with my mom and going back over Meka house that Saturday spending a night. This was the 2nd to last weekend we four (Meka, Keke, Rae and I) will all see each other since I was already in school, Meka was leaving for the navy, Keke was going to job court and Rae was getting her life together. After getting my hair done I informed the three about the fight and that Sunday I waited for my uncle Curtis to drop me back off to Akron. As I went back home I noticed all Kandi stuff was gone and shocked she didn't touch any of my stuff and that ended the beef we had between each other. I also had to report to judicial affair where they put me on academic probation for the fight. The 3rd person I had an altercation with Britt-Britt from Youngstown Ohio. Me and her relationship was cool till I felt her boyfriend company was being disrespectful towards me acting like they touched my food and everyone who knows me know I don't play when it comes to my food or money. Not caring that they was watching the game instead of me going upstairs and ignoring the comments I decide to be petty by kicking her company out making them watch the game at their house which was off campus. I knew Britt-Britt was mad yet I didn't care as long as she ain't come at me sideways I did the same and gave her the respect she gave me. We didn't even talk to each other till one day when we decided to put our differences aside and dropped the beef and we slowly did that. We even went back out together going over her boyfriend house party that was rocking till fights broke out and police were called. Since I was drunk, high and on probation, I hid in the basement with Trooty drunk ass till the officers left yet in due time Trooty was going to piss me off and be on my bad side as well. I got the picture that in this lifetime and generation staying in a house with more than yourself let alone four other girls was like watching the tv show "The Bad Girls Club on Oxygen station yet the only difference was we ain't have no security nor was it fake and I was letting my household know I may not be the bad-est but far from a scary bitch and if I had to fight all my roommates one by one to get the picture and respect I needed then I was willing to do it. Shit at the time the female rapper Nicki Minaj was hot with her mixtapes and me being a fan I had all her songs on my phone using them as ringtones and the one I let play the longest was her song "Bad-est Bitch" saying "I been around the world, I still ain't find another girl that can steal my shine, I had my highs, I had my low, but u can never tell me that I am not the bad-est bitch" and I let that shit be known. Back to the story Trooty and I beef started from the fact her 4 finger male company had sticky fingers as I noticed a pop tart from a cup cake missing yet I had no proof of who took what till I found a pop tart wrapper on Trooty futon bed in the living room then to make him look more suspect I noticed another pop tart missing from out my room and since I now only had one roommate I put the blame all on Trooty and our relationship went south and she didn't even know it till it was too late. As a result of my snacks coming up missing I stole her 3$ she had in her purse along with her mp3 player. Next thing I know a few days later my writing book was missing and since no one knew where it was at I took Trooty's and hid it under my bed and when she asked I denied knowing where it was yet later that day she found it and once I realized that I thought I will have to fight yet she never came at me like that. Don't get me wrong we did argue but it didn't take long for the Ra to intervene and afterwards Trooty admitted to me that her friend had by book and after waiting past ten minutes I got my book back finding out the same 4finger boy stole my book only cause he misplaced his but little did they know I was out for revenge. Lucky for me the chance came where the same 4ffinger boy who stole my stuff left his books unattended and as soon as I recognize it I stole both his math and English books and hid them in the kitchen in the bottom cabinet where no one went in. Since all four roomies had gone their own ways and Kandi not being there no more, I barely seen the three and I was find with that. Britt and Kate was always with their boyfriends while Trooty hoe around and I went from chilling with my cousin Scooter to getting high either by myself or with my classmates to hitting the student union with other students who I met along the way. I even did my anger management program giving to me by my judge thru my school. The last weekend Meka, Rae, Keke and I was together like the four set if off girls we all went to Meka party at Applebee's restaurant along with her family and friends. As Rae Keke and I sat at one table Meka walked around talking to everyone. "Kid" even came thru with his mom who sat behind us. For the 1st time "kid" and I got caught playing footsie underneath the table thanks to Meka yet I peeped Rae and "Kid" not speaking like they used to. Even though I knew "Kid" had other females something about him I still liked. That night after the party we went on country lane to some dude's house to drink and smoke along with Marcy another friend of Meka and we all spent a night there. I fell asleep on everyone including the man that was nibbling on my arm while both Meka and Keke fucked some niggas in the back room. Waking up the next morning I left going back to Meka house to say my goodbye and that night I caught a ride with a friend going back to Akron getting ready for school the next day. As the month of October went past I kept my distance far as my roommates, Rae came up to visit, me for the weekend of sweetest day and Tev decide to be in a relationship with me thanks to Rae thinking Tev wanted her over me. Other than that I did my school work even going to a musical synonym which I enjoyed minus the wrong dress code I had worn during the event a bitch stayed high throughout that month. I even took a trip to Cedar Point with some students from my school and after getting on the 1st ride my phone fell out my pocket and fell somewhere along the way. After waiting for a week I got a replacement phone and I was back cool. As November rolled around things seem to be cool yet on this day after meeting my mentor giving to me by the school I got a voicemail I wasn't expecting. On there it was from my mom telling me to call the house to check on Tink and Boogie and to make the tears start coming down is when she said they just got robbed. Running back home I was prepared to catch the Metro bus back to Cleveland yet when I went in the house to pack and leave grabbing all my school books my roommate Kate offered me a ride to Cleveland and I took it going home less than an hour. Going inside the house I walked in to police and my family and after finding out that both my siblings were hiding in the closet underneath a pile of clothes as a nigga in a navy outfit ran thru the house taking things from my granny cam recorder to my mom money to a camera to a t.v I was too pissed that I stormed outside walking down 147 and 146 looking at everybody as a suspect and had a feeling someone knew something. I was even mad that this was my mom second time getting robbed in the house yet after the first incident my mom put bars on the living and t.v room windows and put bars on both doors and since she already had cameras throughout the house plus an alarm system how could it happen again but I found out that because the keys were left in my mom room and her door was unlocked my siblings never got the chance to press the panic button and I'm guessing they were afraid since Tink was 12 at the time and Boogie was 10. I stayed home with them for the next two days doing my school work off the syllabus and I went back to Akron that Thursday just in time to be ten minutes late for my class. Since I missed two in half days the only thing I was behind on was working with my partner on a power point presentation for my oral communication class. The goal was to have a debate team on the topic of our choice one agreeing with the topic while another disagreed. My first partner was doing a topic on adultery her being for it while I was against it and I was bringing out the bible so I was too pumped for my assignment plus I began to like this class as well learning different ways to talk to people yet after setting up my PowerPoint I was informed she switched partners leaving me without a partner yet luckily for me I partnered up with my favorite smoking buddy Ty miss Aka47 and our topic of choice was teenage pregnancy. I'm not gone lie one of the reasons was to get on one of the three girls who didn't like me or Ty ever since she was expecting and another reason was so I can use Chi-Chi picture and take the subject personal since my mom blame me and Tez for the four year scholarship she didn't take since she had two kids which was going to be my main reason of why I disagreed on teenage pregnancy. We also had to show what we can do to avoid it and other facts and since I love projects I knew this was going to be fun. Over the next two weeks I worked with Ty on our project whenever I was free and since we were last to pair up we were last to present our argument. The week of my presentation I was more than thirsty for my turn as I listened to everyone else that Monday, Tuesday and Wednesday and as soon as Friday came around I was too thirsty and happy we were the only ones presenting that day. As I began my argument I peeped one of the three girls that didn't like me start recording me and once I realized the pregnant girl wasn't there I figured she was recording me for her friend yet before I continue I asked the irrelevant girl was she recording me? What pissed me off is when she replied "does it matter" as if nothing was wrong recording me. The teacher made her put her phone away and I continue my PowerPoint ending with one of the cutest pics Chi-Chi took when she was a few months old. As it was time for the questions after I passed out the condoms as my visual part of the presentation, I started answering questions yet before I could answer the third question I was interrupted by the third girl who didn't like me saying " I know u see my hand up" as if I didn't. As I told her to wait her turn she cut me off saying "fuck that I'm from 99thnorth Blvd. and I replied "bitch I'm from Kinsman which was across town from North Blvd. Just then she got up out her seat and I got from behind my table in front of the class ready to fight yet thanks to the students people were holding both of us back while others ran out the class. Same time I see my partner Ty calling the other girl who was recording me out saying "I want to fight you". As clueless as the other girl look Ty wasn't backing down. Just then I see another teacher coming in telling my teacher that she called campus security and since I was on probation still and now on academic probation from visiting Judicial affairs I grabbed some of my stuff and ran to my house having Ty follow me and meet up with Scooter at my house where we all got high in the basement calming down and scared that the police was looking for the two of us. Since it was a Friday Ty and I chilled that whole weekend at my house going to school that Monday morning walking in the classroom high as a kite. Things seemed cool yet when we went to our oral communication class the teacher wasn't there plus the lights were out. As we set there several minutes I noticed me and the other three girls who was about to fight all got voicemails to go back to judicial affairs where I see the same guy. Since my 1st visit I was put on academic probation yet on this visit I was told that I was kicked out the class along with the other three plus after this semester I was getting suspended the whole next semester and going back home was a bitch and it made me cry after I was in my bedroom alone. I now had to figure out living arrangement and I was not going back to live with my mom. Since I had a short time before winter break starting dec10 I couldn't find a spot in Akron so I was fucked. Since thanksgiving break was that week I went home after finishing my work up from Tuesday since I only now had two classes to complete. Going to my mom house that night I spend a night there waking up to go over Neicce house where I chilled with her lil brother who wanted to fuck me and spend the night waking up the next day celebrating thanksgiving with them. This thanksgiving though I was bond to be thankful for something extra. Waking up I got a call from "Kid" telling me he was on his way to pick me up. Doing the usual riding around like we did plenty times before our conversation he randomly pulled over got out the car to my side and started giving me head. I don't know why he did it and I don't know why I let him but I can tell you I came in his mouth unexpectedly. As many times I was interrupted by Neicce calling me seeing where I went, I had "Kid" drop me off back at her house and as I walked in I walked in on a smoke session and a bitch got high followed by drinking and chilling with some friends of hers then going back to my mom house that night babysitting Neicce's baby boy while she went out. The next day I chilled with my mom for a minute before going back over Neicce's house where I spent another night waking up that Saturday morning headed to the west side to visit Mz. Trouble on business. After talking to her I came up with the plan to move in with her for now and I'll figure everything out later. That night I spend the night at the trap house only this time I barely got some sleep. Due to an altercation between Mz.Trouble and the land lord's daughter the police was called out and after another long story the officers left but not before trying to kick me out yet since I stayed in Akron I had no choice but to stay another night there. Going back to school that following Monday I realized it was only two weeks of school left in other words it was final week the next two weeks. That whole first week I did my work, turned it all in and did my finals that Friday spending my last weekend in Akron. I also got a call from Coco letting me in on Ced who is Chi-Chi father stealing my bank card cashing out. I then called and reported my card stolen and had my account frozen. I went with a couple of students and went out that weekend smoking, drinking and dancing my ass off one last time. That following Monday I spent that whole week off campus going to Turtle house to Nika house where I spent my last two days there. I even turned in my books in for cash including the two books I stole from Mr.4finger guy and got some cash back. I also had to find a way back to Cleveland and nether side of my family helped let alone did shit for me instead Coco and his 38year old friend name "E" who liked me plan to come to Akron to bring my stuff back to Cleveland. Waking up the morning of December 10th I rushed back to campus to meet Coco and his friend. Meeting them at my house, I watched as they loaded "E" truck with my stuff along with some of my roommate's stuff. I didn't care nether did I stop them. They went from taking Kate rug mat to her cover and other petty things yet I personally took all of Trootty dishes. Since I was the first to leave I took the opportunity to fuck with Trooty by taking her shit just like she let her friend take my stuff. I even left several of my stuff behind including all my schoolwork besides the writing essays we did in my writing class. After giving my Ra my house keys I hopped in the truck with Coco and "E" and we hoped on route 2 headed towards Cleveland smoking a few blunts on the way. Just as I was outside of Akron my heart began to ache as I started feeling sad, angry, hurt, and confused, undecided on my future and much more. Going back to Cleveland wasn't the plan yet going back to my mom house where it all started wasn't an option in my book so I had no choice but to play my fucked up hand of cards I was dealt the best way I can......

Chapter2

Going back over Mz.Trouble house was like walking into her house in May of 2010 minus Ced and his baby mother. Since CoCo found out that Ced stole my bank card he had his two cousins who are brothers Joe being the oldest and Chris being the youngest and both of them beat Ced ass then kicked him out the house. Their replacements were more of CoCo friends plus Joe stayed there too on the days he didn't go over his baby mother house down the street. After unloading my stuff I stayed in the house babysitting Chi-Chi, her play sister Megan and their play cousin Sammy. To be honest I didn't know what I was doing nether did I have a plan and I was angry that I was back in Cleveland yet I took it day by day as I stayed on the Westside with Mz.Trouble for literally ten days before we moved. Since it was a trap house all we did was get high and it stayed like that throughout that day yet I wasn't digging that house and its many problems. For starters these bitches ain't have no heat on and by its now winter the house was cold minus the three space heaters we had around the house including leaving the oven on so it was warm in the kitchen. The house also consists of broken windows covered in plastic so the sound of the plastic as the win blow was a sound that didn't stop. Then I was hipped that they illegally cut on the lights, having certain lights work around the house. The most fucked up part about my ten day stay was that we couldn't take showers because of no hot water so I would have to go down the street to Coco cousins in law house name Careem just to take a shower and a bitch was still too uncomfortable to take a shit so best believe I constipated myself for the first week I was there. Finally moving out we moved from the Westside to 93rd in Steinway staying on the second floor while the landlord and her daughter who was expecting her first kid stayed on the 1st floor. As far as Mz.Trouble and I, we didn't lift a finger and after everything was in the new house "E" had set my bedroom up including unpacking my clothes and shoes. Staying in a two bedroom house was way better than us staying on the Westside and that night I let "E" eat the box and fucked him that night. At first I didn't want to because of the age different then he stayed with his baby mother yet after Mz.Trouble talked me into letting him hit, I let him "E" hit and after we finished I waited till his baby mother came to pick him up. I let "E" hit again that charismas and afterwards I stopped at my mom house to pick up something and spent Christmas with Coco and his people meeting Marry who is Careem little sister and her family. Even though I was in a relationship with Tev I didn't take that seriously nether was I planning to let him hit no time soon. Our relationship was based on a lie form him thinking I was still in Akron to him thinking he was the only one I was talking to. I even lied to my p.o I still had to see downtown and had him think I was still in school not letting him know about my school history yet I did complete my anger management classes before I left Akron. Ending the year of 2010 I partied with Mz.Trouble and Coco and his people bringing the New Year at Coco people house off 105 where I shot the same gun Chi-Chi had to drinking and geeking and Mek-mek was right along with us since she was on christmas break coming from Youngstown University. Two days later I got that call from "Kid" and after the convocation I was planning on letting him hit not caring that Tev is his friend yet I was nervous and shy but Coco got me high with the weed I never paid for and by the time "Kid" got to my house I was ready yet I had to push myself to get started. As we both did oral sex on each other I felt good and what was better was when "Kid" inserted his pennies in me. At first I felt uneasy and uncomfortable yet it turned into pleasure as he stroke his ego over and over again till I had enough and fell asleep for a second before kicking him out after the transformer movie came off. After that day I felt a little different and slowly came to realize this was a game of sex that I was willing to play. Over the next week in a half Mek-mek Mz.Trouble and I went out to hit the clubs from Earth to another club where the group "Travis Porter" performed they songs from "get naked" to "make it rain" throwing dollar bills to the crowd and best believe a bitch made sure she got a few singles. Things were going good from getting my check situation fixed to drinking and smoking everyday not having to pay a dollar while watching Coco and his many friends play games from domino to 2k10 to just talking shit and all the entertainment was good and funny as hell. The only thing that pissed me off was the fact my mom was mad about me spending my money on what I wanted plus she found out I was staying with Mz.Trouble so she did one of her many stunts and cut my phone off. That still ain't fuck up my days or my b-day for I did the same shit I did every day for my b-day and Mz.Trouble baked me a cake as I walked around in my outfit I wanted to go out in but since the weather was bad I stayed my ass in the warm house having all the bills including cable in my name while Mz.Trouble and I went half on the rent paying 225$. As the days went on I began babysitting Chi-Chi plus two more babies during the day yet I never complained since I stayed in the house and as long as they kept me high I was cool with whatever was going on. That February I got a revol phone sharing accounts with Mz.Trouble. That month things changed from CoCo being in jail for two weeks to Juju who I met when I went to Hope High moved in taking Joe place in the living room right along with her son Nasty Nate. I got hipped to random people making crack in the microwave by using Chi-Chi baby food jars. I sat there as they mixed it with the baking soda to having Mz.Trouble sell it to certain people including selling the pills. The only thing that wasn't selling out my house was meth and heroine. I even started watching her kid plus another girl daughter name Dede and her mom name is Shay who I slowly met in due time and never charged no one any form of money to watch their kids. I actually had no problem watching kids ever since my first job I had working for KidzHealth 20/20 and picked up some skills along the way and realize I can interact with kids and all ages thanks to my first two jobs of working around kids. I even got my first two tattoos that I thought I was never going to get thanks to my nigga Tattoo Tom. I also met my only sugar daddy J-Mose who took me by surprise after him and "E" was arguing over one disrespecting the landlord so to stop further commotion I jumped in taking J-Mose in the dining room to calm him down yet I didn't have to talk to him. Instead he stuck his tongue down my throat forcing me to kiss him back and from that day forward he slowly became a man I fell in love with not because of who he was but more like what he can do for me. Every visit he came and I came right along with him and afterwards he will leave me with money and different types of weed he (till this day) grows in his basement. I tried from lemon Kush to bubble gum Kush and I loved the attention he was showing me and I was slowly fallen for him. I don't know why maybe because he was an actual man unlike the guys my age I fucked or maybe he was a father figured I never had thanks to my dad Special. Tez used to be my role model yet he dropped out of school after being involved in the riot to being involved in a shootout with his other gang members cripping it out in WestV with my uncle Spanky. I also realized that our relationship was going down the drain and he wasn't the big brother I fell in love with. Other than that the only father figured I had was with my #1 papa who I seen on occasions and at this time he was recovering well from having a drinking stage still grieving over my granny's death 11years ago. Anyways back to my sugar daddy I fucked with him yet business wise and learned some tips he showed me and that was using a nigga for what they can give you and not what they got. Things were going fine. If I wasn't babysitting some kids while the parents did what they did, Mz.Trouble and her friends will come back to the house with a bottle drinking at the house. I even met another one of Mz.Trouble friends name Syn who also has a boy I called jay aka Mr. Michael Jackson. As good things happen so does the bad and Mz.Trouble was the one who made the friendship change forever. Since we never washed at home we will always go to Chagrin Falls where we used Easy-Mac washer and dryer. As Mz. Trouble was using my Gain washing powder I watched her as she watched two loads attempting to wash a third yet I jumped in and stopped her telling her to let me put my clothes in the washer yet she didn't agree which started to piss me off. Ignoring her I took my Gain washing powder and told her she wasn't using my shit till I wash my clothes making sure she wasn't using the rest of my washing powder to wash her, her daughter, and her boyfriend's clothes as if she paid for the washing powder. Getting mad she slapped me in the middle of my conversation and just as she did that all I remember is throwing the butter knife I had in my hand at her followed by me punching her and I blacked out again. All I do remember that night was lying in the snow till someone grabbed me taking me in the house where after I calmed down Mz.Trouble wanted to talk to me. Even though we had our talk afterwards the only person I cared for was Chi-Chi who I loved over the weeks and little did Mz. Trouble know our relationship was never going to be the same and she will tell you herself that as of Feb 28, 2011 at 9:32pm that bitch was and still is dead to me. The reason I said that is because in a friendship there are limits you just have to respect and not cross over yet she didn't care and since I only fight for three reasons she violated two of them and I had to let her know just because I have one hand I'm not tolerating her or anyone else bus since I had dealt with my mom and her issues. Leaving from Chagrin the next day I packed week worth of stuff and headed to Akron to chill with my old classmates. I missed the college life and wanted to go back so bad yet I couldn't so the least I could do was visit on campus once a month acting like I was still in school. Going back to Cleveland the second week of March the hoe of me came out the box for one week straight no lie. That whole week I fucked four different niggas and neither of them was "Kid" or his friend Tev. The first nigga I fucked which is the first night of me coming home was "Kid" older brother J yet he wasn't as good as I expected so I stopped him in the middle of it and kicked his ass out. As soon as he left the laughing started and all the people that were in the house from BigB to Mal to Juju to several more people began roasting him drinking that night. Juju even had us recorded on her laptop of me and Big B freestyle and I honestly don't remember what I said since I was too drunk but from the feedback I could rap talking shit while drunk and if it was a winner I would of won the battle between the two of us. The next day I fucked another one of Coco relatives name Bill giving him them faithful back shots. The third day J-Mose came by giving me head and leaving me with money and weed. The next day Mz.Trouble, Juju Shay and Syn stayed at my house as we bought a bottle and got drunk at home playing on Shay stripper pole. Since Shay is a stripper she did her stripper moves and always kept her pole up on my house in the living room while Syn and Juju had sex for money yet Syn was the only bitch that was making real money fucking with the niggas she fucked with. Any who as we all was drunk we realized Mz.Trouble was too drunk thinking she was going to vomit. She called her friend Al-Be and his crew to slide threw yet since I only met him once at Mz. Trouble baby shower I didn't trust him coming in the house knowing Mz.Trouble was too drunk and since Coco was out in Charging falls making money we had the house to ourselves passing out wherever we fell asleep at. The next day after sobering up it was planned for me to babysit yet me and Juju was about to fall out about me giving her 5$ on a bottle as if I was going to give her any money after all the times I watched her son. Instead we all packed up in two cars having me and Shay ride with Syn while Mek-mek Mz. Trouble and Juju rode in the other car having RoRo (Coco cousin) follow us to the 93rd liquor store where they picked up four random guys and all four cars went to Country Lane where the party was about to begin. Bringing Shay stripper pole with us we sat up and started drinking and geeking listening to RoRo Pandora radio. At first things were friendly drinking and dancing besides Mek-Mek, and I started feeling myself. The first thing that pissed me off that night was Roro and I doing a dummy mission going back to my house not realizing till we got there that no none had the keys so after driving back to Country Lane we decide to stay not going back to my house. What we walked in though as we came back was something I wasn't expecting. I saw Mz. Trouble fucking a nigga while Syn was doing the same and I didn't even know where Shay dipped of to. Then as minutes went by I walked in on Juju and Syn sucking Roro dick in the laundry room at the same damn time. Everybody was doing something expect Mek-mek and I. As everyone was going up and down the stairs walking around naked besides Mek-Mek, I caught Syn fucking Roro in the bathroom to Mz. Trouble giving back shots to another nigga. As the orgy was going on in Syn room all four kids were next room over doing who knows what yet the party was interrupted thanks to Nasty Nate coming out the room. I don't know what started the argument between Mz.Trouble and Juju but since I see Mz. Trouble swing on Juju I followed hitting Juju since she pissed me off before the party even started. Of Corse the others came to separate the three of us. Still heated I followed Juju around the house talking shit and the guys thought it was all fun and games little did they know I was dead ass serious. Mek-mek was now telling me to calm down and the only way I could have done that was leave the house. Since I was already in Country Lane I called Lil Mace and had him meet me since "Kid" gave my number out to both his brothers. Going outside I got frustrated when I couldn't find the way out of the parking-lot, so I literally sat behind a random car till Mek-mek found me and walked with me to meet up with Lil Mace. After I got in his house I don't remember what happen neither can I say what I did and what I didn't do but I can tell you honestly I remember telling Lil Mace I was horny and was sitting on top of him with my clothes still on but for the life of me I don't remember shit that visit but waking up almost 6:00am going back to Syn house where the orgy was still going on and poor little Mek-mek was all alone downstairs while Syn was eating both Juju and Mz.Trouble pussy and Juju doing the same and everybody fucked everybody. Finally going home after 8am I noticed my bra strap was loose and the 5$ that was in my bra was gone. A few days later Coco came back and the house stayed pack. I even let "E" hit one last time just for the fun of it and still had my two to three time visit a week with J-Mose little did I know they both knew I was fucking them both thanks to Coco and his big ass mouth yet nether was my man and as long as Tev ain't know I was cool. Coco was only hear for a few more days before going back to Chagrin Falls and back to the slut ways we all had and since Mek-mek was going back to school it was just the five of us. Mz. Trouble invited Al-Be and his group over and we all chilled having convocations and the only person who was getting some action that night was Mz.Trouble. A few days later "Kid" came back over yet I didn't fuck him. Instead I left with Marry going over her house to wash my clothes and to drink. Coming back home I babysat the same four kids., assuming they was coming right back these bitches didn't come back till after 4am that morning and all came back but Syn who I found out later that day that was in jail for an open container ticket and like a girl about her money she had one of her many male friends bail her out and straight to my house she went. Since her phone was left in a guy's car who was parked in front of Syn car at the time of the arrest thanks to Mz.Trouble leaving it in the guy's car they came over four deep and the party began after I came back home to a house full of niggas plus the five females that was in the house. All nine of us started getting to know each other and since they had liquor I gladly took the offer of drinking since I was already drinking. As soon as the liquor was gone I left with Syn and two guys to go to an after hour spot where the dude bought more liquor and just as I was coming in the house I seen Mz.Trouble leave my room with the dark skin guy. The whole time all the kids was in the other room so I wasn't mad of Mz .Trouble being in my room yet I would be salty if she fucked on my bed. As more liquor was being poured the party continue till the lights came off and everybody had someone to fuck yet Shay didn't fuck no one and afterwards the party continued bringing another dude to the party and we chilled with the niggas from Morris Black projects. Since it was now 7am Mz. Trouble was slowly kicking them out one by one. Still talking shit on how we all were lil girls I let them have they fun but as soon as it was time for them to go I followed one dude name Juice in the hallway where I gave him a quick blow job and when the guy Mz. Trouble fucked came in the hallway I didn't stop sucking Juice dick instead my hoe ass decided to give his friend an example of my head game just because I slowly got the hang of it and as soon as their three minutes were up I went in the bathroom to brush my teeth but when I came out the bathroom I knew I was the topic of conversation. At first I didn't get the joke when they kept saying too hot to handle till I realized that those words were written on my shirt and till this day I go by that name and only a few know the 2hot 2 handle story unless you're reading this book then now u know the 2hot 2 handle story. Not long after they left did CoCo came in waking up the whole house looking for Mz.Trouble phone. They relationship was pissing me off. They went from fighting, to me breaking up a fight getting hit in the process to the many arguments they had throughout the short vast we stayed together. Before the month ended more things changed from having Shay move in to me getting another tattoo adding my aunty and great papa name on the same arm I put my granny name at. I even signed up to get my own food stamps and medical and since I did that my mom was even more pissed since now her food stamps were cut a little. She didn't even let me get my Birth Certificate nor social security card so I had to get it myself. Since I had proof that I wasn't staying with my mom by the ending of March I had my food stamps even though I didn't have all my paperwork I had a set date in April to turn it all in till then I had to get my stuff. Since the social security card was free I didn't have a problem getting it but I had to pay for it and my sugar daddy gave me the money to buy it. Going downtown I patiently waited as the clerk was printing out my birth certificate but when he gave my Id back he explained to me that my name wasn't in the system. Looking at him crazy I told him to look again and don't tell me I'm not a American citizen knowing I went to jail, walked the stage and my hospital records all had the same name yet he came back to his desk and told me my name wasn't on here and asked me for my father's last name to see if he can pull it up that way. Thinking it was impossible he came back and gave me a print out with my same first and middle name yet I had an extra middle name plus a different last name. Still not believing him I assumed it was an April fool jokes since it was April 1st yet when I asked him was he joking with me he said "sorry miss but I don't know you to be joking with you" and as fast as those words escaped his mouth, tears started to escape my eyes. I felt like my whole life was now a lie and how nether of my parents could tell me something this big yet simple rather my name was changed or not. After Nikki calmed me down I went to ask more questions about my name and I received a paper with both my parents signatures and notice I had my father's middle and last name yet neither parent told me so I was too pissed. Going back to the house I was greeted with a house full of people and their kids not knowing I was slowly watching they asses. It was bad enough I had to watch the same four kids plus Mal and Coco daughters plus Marry asked me to watch her three leaving me with nine kids in the house. Marry gave me some liquor and weed while I received nothing from no one else and little did I know everyone who was in that orgy from Roro to Mz.Trouble had the same STD and the 1st to find out was Juju who told no one but when Syn found out she had the other two girls and Roro get tested and treated for the same STD they all had. After finding that out my patience was running short since I had to wait for the parents yet after I fed them and gave them something to drink then as soon as Marry came to pick her three up I left with her catching the last bus to Akron. That night I went out to the Interbelt drunk as fuck and that night was too drunk as we all piled in a van with no seats and the way the driver was driving and doing to much as he hit the corners hard having us all fall over each other in the back of the van as his drunk ass went to Taco bill to order a

McTaco as if he was at Taco Bell plus Mc Donald's. That next day we sober up and went back out that night to a bar call Adam Street where we had a blast. Staying there for another week in a half we partied getting drunk and since I was the only one who smoke weed I was geeking by myself plus the little weed I brought I sold to the other neighbors staying in the five bedroom house in Akron. After I done a lot of partying and drinking I went back to Cleveland where I did the same shit I did different days. I partied at home the days I stayed there and other days I chilled with either Nikki or Shard going over Shard boyfriend house at the time fucking his brother who I just met. The only reason why I let him hit because he was talking shit and so was I little did we both know we could back it up and we did by fucking in the bathroom before I went home that night and that boy felt good stroking me as I bend over the bathroom sink giving him them back shots yet that was only a onetime thing for the both of us. Going back home I took advantage of all the freedom, getting stone and since it was now April these niggas had me drinking every day and yes the good days outweighed the bad. As 4/20 came around we know we was going to kick it this time going back to Chagrin falls for a three day party Easy Mac (who is Roro baby mama) was throwing. The first night was the best. Easy Mac kept us drunk my making strawberry margaritas while blunts were being passed around. Shay even brought her stripper pole out for people to dance on it and the house was packed with people from Chagrin Falls. The second day was cool as people were getting up the party started again yet Mz.Trouble fucked it up again. Sitting down on the couch sipping on Margaritas next to Juju I peeped Mz.Trouble running down stairs and the look on her face she was pissed. Looking from me to Juju to Shay Mz.Trouble decided to slap me. Even though I was drunk my reflex kicked in and I got up punching her in the face from the living room to the kitchen where I fault her in a corner going in a circle around the house the same time I accidentally hit both Roro and Juju with my beads I had hanging around my neck as Tom, Roro and others was pulling me back separating me from Mz.Trouble and after I calmed down I was back at the party geeking and drinking till the next day where the party was still going yet we left that afternoon going back to Cleveland.

Mz. Trouble and I relationship was distance just like Tez and I relationship. Going back home I found out the reason for me getting hit and what pissed me off it was the wrong person that she hit. Things changed even more before April was over with from Juju moving out to me chilling with Nikki to me linking back up with Yoyo going to her house where she now had two kids plus CeCe who is Mz. Trouble sister came by and I chilled over there taking Chi-chi with me sometimes. I barely spent a night and I was slowly coming to the conclusion that after my lease was over that I will be moving out since things weren't the way I wanted to be. I also got tired of her leaving the lights on to finding out after giving Coco 200$ to put on the bills he did who knows what with the money nor did no one pinch in on the bills that was in my name. After talking to Yoyo about the situation she offered me her house yet I didn't take the deal till a week later after coming from my papa Toby house I was planning on Mz. Trouble to do my hair after waiting on her for a while. When she finally got home with Syn and two guys she changed the way she talked to me as if I wasn't going to peep it or say anything about it. As I was getting ready for her to do my hair she cut me off with "I'm a need 20$ is you want me to do your hair" and as soon as she said those words I flipped again. I felt like how the hell did she have the balls to charge me after I done watch her and her friend kids since December nor I wasn't about to pay her for a half as job hair do so after being on the phone with Yoyo I packed my bag to leave to go to Akron plus my hair stuff and off to East Cleveland I went and Yoyo did my hair that night. After the convo about where I was going to rest my head I took Yoyo up on her offered. Yoyo gave me the news of her still talking to Nitty who was also a friend of Tev and that they were still talking on the phone after they ran into each other after one day of coming with me to Mountview to get something from Meka when she came in town. I also had just broken it off with Tev for no particular reason just the relationship wasn't real from the beginning. Planning to go to Akron that next night my plans changed thanks to Yoyo. The day I was supposed to leave, Yoyo asked me to watch her kids while she and Nitty went on their first date seeing "Fast 5". Planning on leaving that evening Yoyo talked me into leaving the next day cause Nitty and his friend was coming over and we was going to do the same shit we did every visit which was drinking long island ice tea and getting high only this time it wasn't like before when me Cece and Yoyo will chill with Kd and Junebug Ed sometimes having Mz. Trouble and Al-Be since they are part of Al-Be click and we all fucked in her house. Any who this time it was Nitty and his friend that I didn't know who it was till he got here; drinking on Chardonnay. I then seen Nitty walk in the door with Cliff and as soon as I realized who he was I instantly got mad that he knew what he was doing knowing him and Meka had history he knew I wasn't fucking him or so I thought. Confused on what to do I took the ride with Angie to the store to get that long island ice tea just to tell her that Cliff was trying to fuck me. Even though Meka was getting married I still cared about how she will feel even though the night they first fucked I was supposed to come over and hook up with him yet I didn't go so Meka jumped on it and I could care less. Anyways going back to Yoyo house Angie left leaving the four of us to drink and smoke and since I knew both already I was talking shit as usual while Nitty and Yoyo enjoyed their own company a little too much. Then these fuckers went to fuck while me and Cliff was in the living room and this nigga had me feeling awkward then the unexpected happen when the nigga started sucking my breast licking my nipple and I don't know it was the liquor or I was horny but it felt good as fuck and long story short we fucked that 2x that night and as soon as morning hit I went on the first Metro bus headed to Akron where I spent mother's day with my classmates and other friends drinking, smoking, and clubbing or bar hopping. The last two days I was there we went to Summit mall and I only hit up JcPenny and seen my one classmate working in the food court and we all chilled at another friend house where we got drunk listening to music laughing over stupid shit. Going back to Cleveland I visited my old house one last time getting my stuff and moved my stuff to Yoyo house putting all my shit and her closet. I also was informed of the shit Mz. Trouble was going thru. For starters she and Coco broke up, then Shay moved out after I left falling out with Shay, BigB , Juju and since the landlord who stayed downstairs only like me she fell out with Mz.Trouble so after I moved out the landlord kicked her out as well taking her to housing court.

Staying at Yoyo house was cool for the time being paying her 100$ for rent this month yet I didn't stay there every night. Someday I chilled with Nikki spending a night at her people's house and even spent a night at my mom house only because Scooter just moved back in town and Tez came in town so it was our lil version of fun getting fucked up. The days I did stay home I made it worth my while yet my stay wasn't that long. All good things always come to an end in this lifetime. The good days I had been fun though. Somedays Mz. Trouble would bring her friend Al-Be over with his crew and we chilled all fucking but Yoyo since she was starting a serious out of nowhere relationship with Nitty to Nitty coming over bringing Cliff dumb ass with him and since I fucked him already it wasn't easy for me not to fuck him especially since we was gone off that long island ice tea and geeking out. One time I did a sex tape thanks to Yoyo recording us as I was giving him back shots the same time he doing a Superman dance with the stupid expressions on his face to his shaking of the head from side to side as I was sucking his dick the whole time Yoyo and Nitty watching and recording and I ain't even know it. My sugar daddy even popped up 2x just to give me weed and money one time dropping food off from Hot Sauce Williams for me and Yoyo ass that he didn't even know. The rest of May was cool but as not even seven days into June did everything go downhill for Yoyo Cece and revenge for Mz. Trouble.

Chapter 3

Soon as June hit things went south as things were heating up between Cece and I. At first I never had a problem with Cece. She aggravated the fuck out of me but I ain't take it to heart yet when I noticed her going back and forth with Yoyo and I about he say she say shit telling Yoyo I had a problem paying my part of the rent yet I already paid it for one and for two it was a lie and that pissed me off and June6, 2011 all hell broke loose. Pissed off I finally set the record straight calling Cece out in her lie yet what pissed me off was she was acting clueless to what I was saying so I left out Mz. Trouble house since she now just moved across the hall from me and Yoyo and went back to the kids party she threw for her daughter. After the party things went downhill. Aggravated from earlier slowly but surely a fight was coming. As the partied ended the house was just left with Yoyo, Nitty and myself till Cece, Mz. Trouble and Toby came and things changed. This time Cece fucked up. Bringing up the same topic Cece started to piss me off again and let them tell it I punched her first starting the fight. So much anger had built up in me and lashed out on her whipping her ass with my one hand putting her in a corner. Just as I was beating her ass Yoyo decides to jump in pulling me down to the floor causing Cece to be over me punching me yet a bitch was still swinging my one hand even biting her hand. Of Course the fight was broken up yet the tension in the room was still there and the b.s was still happening. At the same time I thought about the convo me and Mrs. Ann had a few days earlier and realized what she was saying was coming to happening. Mz. Trouble tired decided to act tough and join the commotion by running her mouth follow by two punches in the face. I got up about to fight her yet I peeped Cece getting up as if she was coming my way. Just as I stopped moving so did she and allowing Mz. Trouble to talk shit same time Yoyo had the nerve to threatening me by asking me did I want to go outside with her meaning do I want to fight her. Since the beef wasn't with Yoyo I didn't think about fighting her yet our bond changed after that day forward. I felt since I knew her the longest our bond should have been better than that yet she showed her true colors. I really don't remember the whole night but words were getting tossed and since I now stayed there I had nowhere else to go. Then out of nowhere I hear Toby voice threatening me with a gun saying "I'll go get my gun and shoot you" as me and Mz. Trouble was arguing. As he left out Mz Trouble left with him and he never came with the gun yet I lost respect for him because he was threading my life and I made sure Tez knew who he was just in case I was to get shot. Long story short as things calmed down Angie came to pick me up and take me to her house spending the night there since I was now kicked out Yoyo house having nowhere to go and still wasn't going   back to my mom house. The shit I went through I said I would never go back there and I meant that unless I was desperate and after all I went through I wasn't as desperate as I needed. The next day after talking to my mom I went to meet up with Nikki and her friend and the three of us met my mom over Yoyo house to get my shit but not till an argument was popping off almost fighting but do to someone calling E.C police they were there three cars deep. As the officers let me get my shit I took Yoyo old cell phone and left dropping my stuff off at my mom house using her van and I chilled with Nikki and her friend at Nikki people's house for a few days then started chilling with her friend Bri at her parent's house and spent my summer going back between both places for the two weeks. Soon as Yoyo found out about her old phone was missing she called me and after lying about who took it I have it to her after receiving 40 punk ass dollars out of the 175$ I just gave her for the one week of that month. That started the fallout between Nikki and I thanks to Yoyo doing he say shit however the fucking story went. Just because I didn't let her or Bri in on me lying about who took the phone Nikki got in her feelings and we ain't been cool since. I then just chilled with Bri at her parent's house. I popped up at my mom house grabbing clothes taking a shower and spent a night 2x that month. I even was avoiding my papa Toby lying to him one time I had the pink eye and because of that I had caught the pink eye not even a week later to having my mom ride past him just as he pulled up to my mom house yet I finally gave him and his family an actual time to chill with them other than parties that July 4th weekend of 2011. Meeting three cousins of mines for the first time we went to a block party where papa Toby grew up meeting his youngest sister Daisy and my Uncle Fuddy's father who stayed down the street from Yoyo. That night we went to Momma T house seeing my siblings E-boo and man man and their two order sisters Lisha and Nita who was the oldest. From that day forward I went back to Momma T house chilling with Lisha and Nita since we all had one thing in common which was getting high and since I was almost off probation for good I was too happy to feel free. I even talked back with Tev leading him on like "Kid" lead me on still not planning to fuck him. I even chilled with him for a sec yet I didn't plan on ever fucking him....... yet. That whole July I kept myself entertain by seeing what others were doing in their lives. I even fuck this nigga I met off of Facebook little did he know it was a onetime thing for him as well as the other guy I fucked after using him for a bottle of wine and a few blunts and even though he was good I wasn't giving him my real name nor did I let him or the other guy hit. When August came around Lisha let me move in her house so I grabbed certain shit and left the rest of my stuff in my mom garage and days at Lisha house was fun. We stayed high meeting her 30th friends from Bama who I no longer like to peaches who I fuck with in a distance. We would literally stay high and at night it was a party at Momma T's house and when I say party I mean people, drinks weed and spades on the table paying music since my papa Toby, my dad and other family members came through I included that as my dad side of the family since my dad was once married to Momma T having two kids. Speaking of kids rumor was her have a 4th child who I never met yet. I was also looking for a one bedroom house having my dad come with me yet it was hard to find a place to stay and by my being 19 at the time people didn't want to lease to me. Lucky for me after having a convo with Lisha she offered her home to me right along with my uncle Faddy so I took that chance and kept it pushing. I only bought a few things to Lisha house and even though I was now house hoping I was still planning on moving by myself not letting no one know my plans since people were now seeing me struggle. I even linked back up with Dai-dai and chilled with her and Moe from time to time. As soon as August 16th hit I went to my last court date and after I left I went straight on 30th and bought an Oz smoking with people from Lisha to Bama to my dead to Lisha friend but I mainly smoked that shit up less than 1week.

That's how happy I was to be free from something I didn't do. Since my suspension was over with I decided to sign up for school again and as bad as I didn't want to go to Tri-c I decided to sign up for classes little did I know I couldn't use my financial aid till I got my transcripts both from Bryant and Stratton college and Akron university and since I past the deadline it was too late to do that semester so I decided to re enroll spring of 2012 till then a bitch kicked it with Lisha and the crew from getting high going to the show seeing final destination 3D to getting high all night talking shit to party at my aunty house several times. They even had a thing call family fun night that my family on my mom side ain't do and I'm not gone lie I was having fun and even though Lisha not my real sister our bond was special in my eyes but the same shit that make you laugh will make u cry.

Chapter 4

After coming back from Kennywood with my mom I got a text from Lisha basically saying she wanted me to leave little did she know I was looking for houses already not taking her up on her offer bout moving to a house with her with her two kids I came to love as if I had a niece and nephew. I adored Pooder and Jaja with they bad self. Not explain what the situation was about, I waited till I got to her house to see what the problem was. I felt like since my uncle Fuddy stayed with us as well paying her 25$ rent five times the amount I shouldn't pay as long as it was food and weed here plus I bought household items, paid her to do some micro plus letting her and Nita borrow money that they never paid me back to letting her use my free bus pass going with her places yet she wasn't satisfied. After talking it out and letting her know she was the last resort since I couldn't stay over papa Toby house nor did my daddy have a house and I didn't want to go back to my mom house she decided to let me stay yet tension was still there. After a week I got another text saying she wanted me to leave. Not knowing why I started asking questions and from what Momma T was saying it was a lot of he say she say shit going on not knowing who was saying yet so to chalk it I packed the little shit I had and left dropping it off at my mom house yet I didn't stay the night instead I went over Bri house chilling with her till I packed one week in a half outfit to Akron. Going to Akron I chilled at a friend house during the day as she went to school and work. As she was out I smoked visiting campus missing the college life and at night we hit the club's one time going to a club called Lux that was packed with white and mixed people with a bar and I had a blast dancing with two white boys at the same time for the 1st time. Going back to Cleveland I came to the solution to move in one of the houses Marry owned off 116 and I was moving Nov 1st until then I was chilling. After staying at my mom house I then left for few days fucking around with Danny (Fry) daughter. Planning on babysitting I stopped over Meka people to buy some weed from her little cousin Man and leave yet both Man and Danny had something else planned. Setting the trap Man asked me to go in on a bottle of that long island ice tea yet when I came back "Kid" had just pulled up and that's when I caught on to what Man and

Danny was doing after I had plan to babysit and meet a different guy yet plans changed and I really didn't have a choice since I still wanted to fuck him even though we only had fucked once. Walking to Man mom house Tev jumps out of nowhere but a tree and bushes wearing all black asking us what we was doing same time I removed "Kid" arm from around my neck distancing myself from him as we walked in the house leaving Tev outside with the crew not wanting him to know his friend "Kid" hit . As soon as the drink was gone and I smoked my weed someone turned the lights off and the fucking began Danny fucking Man while "Kid" got him a quickie. Danny and Man fucked that whole night in the basement and never even stopped even when Tae a friend from the hood came down the basement asking to go to I Hop to Man lil brother coming downstairs and I watched as Danny squirted all over the basement. The next morning I got high with Man mom San and "Kid" dad talking. Fucking "Kid" again this time in Man brother room we chilled the remainder of the day till "Kid" had to leave to go to homecoming with a girl who I soon found out was his girlfriend at the time which pissed me off cause he just cheated on her with me feeling like a sidekick or something. Anyway for the remainder of Oct I chilled with Dai-Dai getting a pierced tongue to tattoos or going over my cousin Misty dad house and I only went home to change clothes. I even visited my new house counting down the days till the day I moved in. Since Dai-Dai wanted to leave home and do her I decided to let her move in with me both paying 225$ for the month of November little did I know I didn't know what I walking into till it was too late. After both of us moved in we found out that there was no furnace thanks to the gas man telling us the reason he couldn't turn on the gas. I was pissed Mary knew this and having us looking stupid as fuck. After telling her about it instead of leaving Dai-Dai and I stayed there with space heater from my mom and Mary. Neither one of us didn't want to go back to our mom's house so we all made it work. I met her boyfriend at the time name Ink and the three of us chilled at the abandon as I call it. We even had the water cut on illegal way yet that ain't technically had nothing to do with me and the lights were cut on in my name so as long as there were lights, water and a way for us to stay warm I was rolling with the punches. Since the fall out with Lisha I wasn't chilling with the whole family and I talked to papa Toby from time to time and since him and my dad stood me up on helping me move I distanced myself from them and thanks to my #1 papa he helped me move not searching the house like he offered. Really I was just too thirsty to have a house I was desperate to have a roof over my head. I also met my dad 4th kid which is a girl Chi-chi age who I instantly connected with and her b-day was seven days before mines. Since Dai-Dai worked at Boston Market during the day I either stayed home or left going over Man house sometime chilling with Tev. As the month went by we survived off a hot plate using it to cook and boil water taking hoe baths in the bathroom. We also had a deep fryer and fried food in there. Since we had two space heaters we kept our rooms warm and the other part of the house was cold so that was our fridge. On her off days we went to the show or over her mom house. Then the unexpected happen......the day I fucked Tev thanks to Man again. Going over Man house Nov29th Tev talked me into seeing him so I took my time getting high and having Man and his girlfriend come with me and we all chilled since the house was all his for the weekend. As I went back in Tev room to watch a movie call "The Battle Of Las Angeles" giving Man and his gf some space yet after being back there I came to check on them and they left leaving me in the house alone with a Tev who been trying to fuck me over a year in a half now. Since he wanted me to stay and I ain't having nothing to do I decided to stay over and that's when the trap to fuck me was set. Slowly but surely he gave me head sliding his dick in afterwards but not till after he said the words "trust me" while lil Wayne "so special" came on and that was the first time I was intimate with a guy I fucked instead of just liking a guy. That night he held me as we slept and I had started feeling something for him and best believe it wasn't his looks. We even went two more rounds during the night leaving hickeys all over my neck and chest and he was the first person to ever leave a hickey on me and for some odd reason I liked the fact that he did that minus the oblivious mark that I fucked someone or was intimate. Giving Marry a few more days she finally had her baby daddy bring the furnace and hook it up. Waiting on the gas company a few days later one came out again to give me more bad news that pissed me the fuck of. Coming from the basement the gas man informed me that it wasn't hooked up right after testing it out. Since I was already mad at Marry for the lights having a shortage causing Cleveland public power making way too many trips, I went off letting my anger get the best of me and fussed at Marry telling her she not getting no money till she fix the problem same time I was deciding to move. After the argument I fucked her house up busting out glass cabinets to the kitchen shelf to kicking both screen and door off the hinges completely and by the time I was done police was called thanks to next door neighbor who happens to be Chi-chi play sister Megan's mom and like I told them "Would you or your kids live here knowing all the problems?" and after agreeing with me they told me different actions I could take if I wanted to stay here still yet since the front door was broke I knew we had to move and three days later we found a house around the corner on 116 in Luke which is a street next to Kinsman. I spent two nights at my mom house before moving in December 16, 2011 where "Kid" broke the house in with me and ass his strokes were deep so was my grip on his back and his body and that boy felt good. I felt like since he ain't care about him cheating on his gf then nether should I yet that doesn't mean I was agreeing with his actions. He was simply setting an example my dad and brother showed me and that was getting all the ass you can and I was somewhat on the same thing. Since none of my family didn't wanted to help me move Toby volunteer moving my clothes to the new house around the corner and moved my bed in the next night. Since the big fallout between Cece and me I slowly talked back to Mz. Trouble after her apologize for her behavior yet even that didn't change shit. On the strength that I love her daughter I let by gone be by gone and as far as Yoyo and Cece I seen they true colors. My first week was cool but little did we know things were going downhill and Dai-dai and I friendship was slowly but surely about to change. For starters thanks to Dai-dai getting caught cheating on her bf Ink with her now baby daddy Chris, I let his dumb ass talk me into letting him have sex with me so it will be in even score not knowing he was just using me to fuck. Of Course when he first suggests it I wasn't for it but as the days went by I let his talking get to me. Scared to tell

Dai-dai thinking she wasn't going to believe me over Ink I took matters in my own hands. Not saying it was right nor till this day am I feeling good about it but as soon as the opportunity hit and I was in my room watching Chi-chi and Dede did Ink took control of the situation. As he let the kids play with Dai-dai toady bears Ink came in my room shutting the door behind him. At that moment I knew what was going to happen and real shit afraid of saying no thinking I could get raped I let him do as he pleased but not without me wrestling with him first putting up a fight till he slammed me on the bed pulling my pants down and once my whole bottom was naked I let him fuck me taking in his dick. I liked the authority he had over me something that both "E" and my sugar daddy did yet I knew it was wrong and wasn't plan on telling no one yet. As the days went by Christmas came around and my plans was to stay at home. Dai-dai had to go to work leaving me in the house yet my day turned out unexpected. Waking up I let Tev come over to give me a holiday special giving him them back shots. The whole time since Mek-mek, Toby, Mz Trouble and Ink were there they had a show yet it was interrupted thanks to the old man who stay next door from me staring at us and since I didn't have blinds it wasn't hard seeing me. Just as we stopped, feeling too embarrassed to finish. Same time Tez was coming thru the door just as I went to the bathroom letting Tev out the door. Scared of what Tez was going to say, I made convo with Tez not trying to feel awkward and him asking me why. Then to make things feel more awkward for me everyone in the house left and I peeped that all the shit both Mz Trouble and Toby talking about Tez and him being a Crip was replaced with friendly gestures. I also let Tez know Toby by face because of the incident with the threat of the gun. Soon as the house was empty Tez let me in on he knew Tev was here for me and got hipped I had sex yet to my surprise he respected it saying I'm grown so he gone let me do what I want but not when he's around and I respected that shit. That day we called Scooter and we spent Christmas smoking and drinking while they played the game and later that night I invited my friend Mz. Phoo and her group of five people and two of them me and Tez new from Hope High and of course Dai-dai and Ink joined in and we turned up at my unfurnished house but since I had carpet it was cool. If I had

~ 38 ~

help moving I would of never had to leave my couch but over the years I got use to leaving stuff behind and taking it as a lost. The next day was the same just lesser people and on the 27th I was back to normal yet I peeped certain shit such as Ink being rude pulling my pants down in front of Dai-dai to pulling Lala who is Dai-dai little sister pants down exposing our panties. He also did little petty shit from playing with my boobs while Dai-dai was in the tub to stealing one of my filter tips mild out my purse as if I didn't hear him take it thinking I was sleep when I was texting Tev laying down. Only two days past and I had had enough with Ink and his ways even after I let him fuck two more times he still wouldn't leave me alone so I told Dai-dai thinking she was going to break-up with him yet she didn't witch made me mad. She claim she wasn't mad but I think she was and the tears proved it and because of that I feel our relationship would be different since I always will regret that fucking her dude shit and I don't think she would ever trust me again and I don't blame her. I even talked to her mom, Tev and "Kid" bout it hearing their views. Ending that year things seem cool and the turn up was at my house inviting Mz.Trouble, Mek-mek, Lala, Toby Ink and Dai-dai and I plus I got to see my little sister Naisha and since her and Chi-chi were the same age they played while we got drunk from playing 10 fingers to just drinking and a bitch got too drunk I barely remember that day, I even missed the fight between my little sister and Chi-chi and from the feedback my little sister won. The next day was a recovery for me as Dai-dai watched the kids for me and as the days of 2012 started they seem cool shit great in my eyes. I met this new freak I call my Mr. Head Doctor and after kicking with him the second night I fucked him playing the Drake "Take Care" CD and his name Mr.Head Doctor for a reason. Waking up the people in my house including Mz.Trouble and Toby I had the ride he wasn't ready for. I even met this nigga Mr.Juju who after chilling before I let him hit and he was better than both Tev and Mr.Head Doctor which mean I was keeping him for a while not really knowing him neither was I trying to get to know him. Me and Dai-dai relationship was cool but ever since I told her about Ink I let it be clear that he wasn't allowed in my house unless she was here. I slowly got hipped to him using Dai-dai for her money thinking he was gone stay here yet I let her do her. By the 14 of January Tev decided to get back with me and that night as we talked about it over texting I fucked Mr. Head Doctor cheating on him not even five minutes in the relationship real shit. It's not like it's my first time cheating but I don't know why I just did it and I like sex and used Mr. Head for money and weed since we both got high. He actually was a cool nigga to chill with plus his group of friends one of them being Tev little cousin who showed me HIS LONG DICK with his 16year old ass and if I had a chance to fuck him I wouldn't be afraid of his length when it was as hard as it was that night I seen it after getting out the tub. Since me and Tev was now in a relationship he came over more often yet that didn't stop me from doing me the ten days we were together till I broke up with him. I went from cheating on him with Mr. Juju to giving Toby's friend a one minute blow job in the hallway closet while Tev was in the bedroom behind the wall where I was at to having him meet my head doctor not knowing that I was fucking him. Actually I thought Mr. Head Doctor would leave after I let him know that Tev was on his way yet he never left and that's how the both of them met and they chilled for a second till Mz. Trouble made it awkward for us telling Toby she couldn't wait to get her second abortion that she was getting the begging of February so we all left having Mr. Head Doctor go his way while I left with Tev. The night before my b-day it changed. There were good times from having a water fight with Dai-dai and Ink to me chilling with him all day and there were bad days such as when he pissed me off breaking my mild by playing too much and having my first makeup sex ever to his ways of him being immature and the childish ways and self-centered ways and after sleeping with Mr. Head Doctor the night before b day and after waking up the day of my b day I broke up with Tev as the many times I did before and really don't know why I did it. See Tev adored me and that's what I loved about him even though he pisses me off he adored me yet I guess it wasn't enough. I spent my day in the house with Mr. Head Doctor who I started to like and his crew and invited Mz. Trouble and Mek-mek and Man came through to slide me some weed in the party started in the kitchen paying spin the bottle for the first time girls sucking titts to boy on girl action yet I was the only person who fucked that night as others besides Mek-mek and Mz. Trouble were licking and sucking on each other just for fun. What's strange is after that next day Mr. Head Doctor left and never came back, I talked to him two days later on my now broke phone but since I got a new phone he didn't have my number and since my old phone was broke I switched from revol to boost mobile getting a blackberry. I felt like I broke up with Tev for nothing and since we wasn't on the fucking level let alone talking barely I wasn't fucking him yet I had my other toy fucks from "kid" to Mr.Juju to fucking my god brother as a onetime thing. Mz. Trouble came offend and since my cousin Trey worked across the street from me at the Family dollar on 116 in Kinsman him and his sister Missty came over including Neisha and we chilled art my house. Just as things were good things were aggravating me till the 16th when Dai-dai and I fell out over a few things and she moved out. For starters she was late on rent still not paying after I paid my half then I notice her giving Ink her money to him or her stealing food that I bought for Chi-chi and since this house ain't have a fridge or refrigerator we had cabinet food and using a cooler for cold things. My mom even used my money to buy me a 150$ nu-wave oven that I thought was a gift when I received it. I was pissed because I could have used that money for a stove she knew I was trying to get. Her bf already stole 10$ from Chi-chi and Toby half a blunt yet what set it off was when I woke up to a dirty house. I woke up seeing my kitchen dirty with dishes everywhere plus trash so I woke up the house including Mz. Trouble since she was there too slowly moving in. I made Dai-dai wash the dishes only to find out she half washed them thanks to Man telling me to check them and I flipped punching holes in the wall in my room and later that day after flipping out on her, I told her she can leave not knowing she was leaving the next night. The next day we was informed about Ced baby and her mom mother died getting shot after Chi-chi little sister died after being only 13months and we went to the funnel a week later. The thing I would never forget at her funeral is the site of her holding her baby in the casket and when her pastor said "everyone has an appointment with death that we can't miss." As the days went by things were cool after I moved Mz.Trouble in. Since my cousin worked at the Family dollar across the street from my house him and his siblings Missty and Niesha came thru and we turned up at my house along with Mz. Trouble and Mek-mek and I had fun yet always when things go good they also go bad and Mz. Trouble was the blame for my madness. For starters because of her Tev and Toby was about to fight over whatever Tev said to Mz Trouble and because I didn't want Tev to get his ass beat I intervene yelling at everybody while punching holes in my wall for the second time kicking everybody out that night. I was already pissed that I took a trip to Akron to get my transcript yet since I didn't pay the student loan back from my mom I couldn't get the transcript I needed to enroll in Tri-c. After that Mz. Trouble managed to piss me off but this time I literally blacked out after being drunk hanging with Missty. I really don't know what started but whatever Mz. Trouble was saying pissed me off causing me to flip and after seeing five smiling faces staring at me on the wall all hell broke loose. After they wouldn't stop smiling everything went black and all I remember was a bloody hand and police there with EMS and long story short I was escorted to St. Vincent hospital on 22nd street where I was released the next morning. Going home I was told I went from punching the wall to breaking glass to missing my granny and many more. As the days went by my mom popped up finding out Mz Trouble moved in while Dai-dai was gone and she was pissed again and I was the one who slowly but surely suffered. At first things seemed cool. Daily parties was always at my house to Mz Trouble inviting Al-Be and his crew came over the nights Toby worked to having a new group of friends that both Mz. Trouble and I fucked along with Al-Be and Kd. Other days I went with Toby and Mz Trouble to chill with his friends all from Lee road. Things were cool and I figured I'll go back to Tri-c and try again not using my transcript and August till then I woke up with no idea how the day will turn out so I went with whatever flow it was on that day. I went from just inviting people over to play cards and Man started hanging with us as well meeting Mz. Trouble, Toby, Mek-mek, even Cece and Toby friends from Iggy to Trap and Lil d to Dope boy who I wasted my time fucking after ten strokes he bust REAL SHIT and a bitch was salty. Yet before the end of March Mz. Trouble and I had it out for the third time with Mz. Trouble. Doing the usual which was get high and whoever came slid through chilling.

Back then I didn't realize my house was a party house nor didn't realize the different people from "Kid" to Dj, who I met through Mz.Trouble who was cheating on Toby bitch ass with three different niggas from Coco to Al-Be, to fucking Mr.Juju to two more and I stayed geeked even popping pills for the first time yet on the next day of after partying at my house popping two pills for the first time that night the ending of the next night I popped two more. Only people were Mz. Trouble, Mek-mek, Man and his two cousins my cousin Trey and Chi-chi was there at every event that popped off at my house. As things were going find Mz. Trouble for the most likely person to fuck up the mood award. Getting upset that I was on my phone as her friend was calling me Mz. Trouble was mad that I didn't let her use my phone. Instead I told her friend to call back she had an attitude as if she paid my phone bill as if she haven't used my phone plenty tines before talking to different niggas. Any who long story short shit hit the fans when she unexpected slapped me in the face and that's when all hell broke loose. As soon she slapped me that anger I had towards her since the shit she did last year I began attacking her punching her multiple times while walking from the living room to the dining room till people broke it up yet I was still angry that I walked around the house punching things from the walls to the glass cabinets causing deep cut in left hand. I was so mad I sat on the porch outside smoking mild in my thoughts out loud and from that day I knew I couldn't let Mz. Trouble stay in the house with me and our friendship wasn't going be the same. After another convo with Mz.Trouble I let go on what happened but wasn't fucking with her how I wanted to fuck with her. I was planning on either leaving or kick her ass out too yet thanks my mom, the next door neighbor and the landlord it was possible. Things went back on track kicking it at my house. Syn even slid through and my dad came through meeting a few people to Roro and his kids were coming. I even met a new nigga I was using him for his money and still fucked with my sugar daddy for his money and weed to having daily as house parties as people call it having my cousins and Man who brought Cliff to his little cousin Shawn and we all had our version of fun every day no lie. Shit even threw a party for my little cousin Niesha at my house. As usual I invited different people over this time

~ 43 ~

inviting Wayne aka Mr. Lil dick over with his group of people which were the same two nephews and a friend but this time I let Toby talk me into letting them all spend the night instead of me kicking them out like I always did.. I met Wayne around the same time I started talking back to Tev but not on relationship terms. The first day Wayne came over he bought a bottle and some bud for Mz. Trouble, Toby and I to leash off of then after I left to fuck Tev who stayed down the street from me while Wayne stayed in Bedford yet was always at a house across the street from mines. Back to the story I had Mek-mek sand Man spend the night as well having a house of ten people in my house including Chi-Chi who was only three at the time. That night I let Wayne masturbate me by rubbing on my click the way Dj taught me when he did. See Wayne wasn't my type since he was a big fat guy and his breathing heavy was a turn off for me. Then to add insult to injury that night as he slept in my bed I used my ass to rub on his dick to picture how long it was yet as I did I managed to feel nothing and took it as he has a small dick nor was I informing anyone about what I knew and didn't want to embarrassed him not knowing how tomorrow was going to turn out. Waking up the next day I guess Toby pumped Mr. Lil dick head a little too much. Then the shit talking started telling me that I couldn't handle him and I wasn't ready to fuck him yet I knew the real reason of why I didn't want to fuck him and Mz. Trouble and Mek-mek knew I was using him for his money playing the girlfriend roll in Mr. lil Dick eyes. Toby and Man even participated in the shit talking by offering me money and pills to fuck Mr. Lil Dick yet the whole time I said nothing till Mr. Lil Dick had the nerve to pull out a magnum gold condom from his back pocket throwing it on my bed telling everyone in the house that he can do 50 pushes with me all day and that pissed me off since I know he couldn't do what he said and I decided to embarrass his ass since his ego was too big for. Since I figured Wayne had a little dick I knew he would be embarrassed getting exposed and since my door had a hole where u can see in my room just like when Mz. Trouble and them seen me and Tev on Christmas. It was a house full including him and his two nephews and his friend plus man and his friends plus Mek-mek, Mz. Trouble and Toby and Chi-Chi was there at every event. Playing two different games of spades I got high knowing I'm funny when under the influence and little did Mr. Lil Dick know he was in for the laugh. As soon as I won three games and a several blunts were past I let Mz Trouble in on the joke and I lead Mr. Lil Dick into the bedroom where I positioned myself in a doggy style exposing my body and he did the same. Since I knew his penis was small plus my sex game was on fleek I knew everybody including Mr. Lil dick crew was watching. After attempting to hit it from behind I then rolled on my back giving him a chance to stick it in yet my laughter was uncontrollable as I bust out laughing after holding my breath and I screamed Mz. Trouble name wiggling from underneath. As soon as I opened my door Toby and Man fell on the floor laughing their asses off and I took Mz. Trouble in the bathroom with me explaining I couldn't go through with it without laughing as I was getting back dress. Toby jumped in the convo telling me I should fuck him now since I made him look bad and that I was wrong for doing that in front of all these people and after the convo I decided to try and fuck him knowing it was going to be quick and me faking it yet when I told Mr. Lil Dick to come back in the room he flipped telling me he was just trying to get his dick sucked and that pissed me off yet I thought it was too funny and let Mr. Lil Dick crack jokes saying I'm a 116th hoe if that was my hood till my pussy stank and other b.s yet I had jokes as well telling him if I was to suck his dick it wouldn't past my teeth confirming his little dick problem to letting him know he just got used by a handicap bitch that he ain't never going to fuck and afterwards I kicked him and his crew out my house letting him know the fake relationship he thought we had was now over. That day me and others who were there will never be forgotten. As April went buy things were going good yet as usual as things were good things were going downhill and I ain't see it coming. There were other good times including parties with my cousins till spending all night with Toby and his crew going from Wal-Mart 4am to learning how to play Casino to go over Trap house all morning watching them gamble. Toby was making moves with Man sailing pills and weed and we had a blast staying geeked chilling with Mz. Trouble, Mek-mek having Chi-chi right by our side while Toby and Man did there thing as their bond grew stronger As usual as things look good it also go bad.

For starters I found out what Dai-dai did thanks to Ink telling Mz. Trouble everything from the reason I never seen my Mr. Head Doctor no more do to a rumor about me fucking his friend who is also Tev little cousin who Lala wanted to fuck so in return Lala started fucking Mr. Head Doctor even though she was only sixteen at the time and her was ten years older than her. I also found out that Dai-dai telling Tev I cheated on him witch explain the Facebook status of Tev calling a girl a hoe and even though I had a feeling he was referring to me I never knew she told on me. Too mad that it was a lie I was madder than me head doctor never told me about it. Confronting Dai-dai about it we almost fault due to I was mad she played me on the rent and for her telling my mom what was going on in my house yet the words she said made me mad at her but not as mad as I was towards my mother. Dai-dai falling in one of my mom hands feeding into her lie Dai-dai told her about me fucking her boyfriend to having Toby over my house selling drugs out my house yet what came out my mom mouth and for Dai-dai to repeat it "that I was now going to have fend for myself" since Mz Trouble and Toby were at my house. Them words hurt so bad that I cried later that night. I also was informed but my uncle Spanky that the landlord and my mom was trying to kick me out the house and to the help of them both plus the next door neighbor who stayed above me it didn't take them long. For starters by Mz Trouble and the lady upstairs were beefing yet everything went cool till the day her house got robbed and since Mz. Trouble was beefing with her the lady upstairs accused of us stealing it and after police searched my house the drama for more deep when she bust out my dining room window after arguing with Mz. Trouble. Telling the landlord it took him two days to re-fix my window the same time he advised me to find another place to live yet I ignored him and kept partying. Both Spanky and Scooter came by drinking whiskey and smoking playing spades back to back and me and Spank won more games than we lost. I even invited Mica from south over to play cards and smoke letting time past me by to even fucking Cliff to my sugar daddy I even let Tev hit again after our talked. Things were cool minus the fact my mom wouldn't give me my whole check thanks to papa Toby he paid my phone bill for that month yet before the month ended me and Mek-mek got into our one and only fight after playing a hand of spades. Doing the usual playing cards, popping pills, geeking and it was just the same group Mz. Trouble, Toby, Mek-mek myself and Chi-chi . Things started off good Mek-mek being my partner yet when this round of cards were dealt shit got real as I was dealt 8spades,2face cards and no diamonds plus three other cards I knew I can make nine books by myself i figured we can make ten books setting Mz Trouble making them lose points playing cards like papa Toby and my dad played yet Mek-mek interrupted my thoughts by poking me in the chest saying "it's all in your chest" as I asked her how many books she had since I knew what I can make yet by Mek-mek poking my reflex was a slap to the face. I honestly thought I didn't hit her yet from the feedback I was told I hit her first. In retaliation Mek-mek hit me back. Thinking she was playing how she always like to play fight I knew this was serious after the third hit follow by her grabbing my leg pulling me closer to her. As she was over me she get to swinging while I was on the floor yet I got up and punches were being thrown back and forth fighting from the wall to the bed all in the room Mz. Trouble slept in. We continue throwing punches till we literally were tired and as the fight ended I went to chill with a friend for her b-day getting high. She can't say she whipped my ass and I can't say I whipped her ass. It took Mek-mek and I a few days to talk again and once we did we picked up where we left off kicking it every day not knowing nor couldn't predict how the day was going to turn out. The same shit we did every day from racing down the street to double dares and the day wasn't complete without liquor weed and pills popping as the month ended. One thing that stood out was the conversation I had with Mrs. Ann and I had regarding my life. Still till this day I can't forget the words "something is going to happen to you but you will be ok at the end of the day. You will find you a place not too big nor too small for just one person. I see you in a one bedroom not quite out the way but not close. Watch who you bring in your house and stop having many friends over and that she see me with one friend coming over". At the time I thought she was talking about fighting or something yet I was soon to understand what she was talking about over the next year. Unfortunately for me it was days away from my downfall and I ain't see it coming.

Chapter5

As the month of May rolled in things was supposed to be the same little did I know I was waking to a rude awakening. Since my mom found out Mz. Trouble moved in with me she did her things first by telling the landlord that I had people moving in my house selling drugs to not giving my money from the SSI knowing I had to pay rent. Waking up on May 3rd I receive my eviction notice for the first time. At the time I was confused of why it was happening and pissed that I was slowly getting kicked out my house and now worrying about where I was going to stay at now and going back to my mom house was not as option. Since me and Meka feel out again for the second time I figured I couldn't stay with her knowing that was the reason for the fall out because she wanted me to move with her and her husband at the time back in February. Thinking of options I came with the idea of leaving Cleveland going to Michigan to move with Tez and his girlfriend not knowing at the time it was all a setup. Tez sold me a dream he couldn't afford. Lying he told me that I can help pay rent in a two bedroom house that's furnished and had two bathrooms and the best part was the bedroom I was sleeping in was going to be sleeping on different floors meaning I had my own privacy to my own bed being there already so I planned on leaving most of my shit here like I always did yet there was a lesson GOD was going to teach me over the next year and had people but my papa Toby thinking I was going to West Virginia till then since I was leaving I felt I was leaving with a bang and the majority time of me being on 116th was straight going to party and fuck as much as I could starting with Dai-Dai bf Ink who became her ex to Tev to my sugar daddy. My plan was to stack up and do my own thing and if it was opportunity to leave I was taking it and the mean time I was going to enjoy the last few days and I only had two weeks I was going to party and had that fuck Cleveland attitude and fuck this house. Since my mom didn't give me my check nor my rent money I went down to social security and changed my payee from my mom to my papa Toby since I couldn't become my own thanks to my mom letting them know I had went to jail and it's only been nine months since I was on probation. Since that was a process I had to wait to get my money from April and May so I was shit out of luck far as receiving my money and that month Spanky paid for my phone bill and bought me a pair of Jordan's. That pissed me of even more that my mom was acting like that for no reason actually because I let Mz. Trouble stay there yet she knew the plan that we want staying for long. Getting off of reality I through random kickbacks and collect weed and money from sugar daddy and getting bud from Man and we kept drinks going with people having a party and Spanky and Scooter came over letting me in on my mom plans and talking to the landlord. Missty even had a party for her b-day at her (who I thought was just a friend yet is her husband on the low) and it was cool till some gay bitch was arguing with Missty and I assuming no one but her sister Neisha and was watching and from the body launches things looked heated yet after the back in fourth talking a fight was about to jumped off as Neisha and I ran to Missty rescue but the drama didn't end well. Make a long story short Missty decided to leave and take the party to her dad house so we all walked off yet the people who was mad at her for I don't know what reason took it upon themselves as we were walking to Broadway did a car past throwing her cake on the ground driving off. As me and my three cousins walked off a random guy walked past and seen it and asked was we cool giving Missty a blue dolphin pill for me and since it was her b-day he gave her some money pining it on her dress and the way she wore that red dress and red pumps said it all. Lucky for Missty soon to be husband came through picking us up at Wendy's, and took us to the liquor store where he bought drinks and drove to Missty dad house listening to Jeezey 103cd where met up with their youngest sibling Dev and Trey came right along my cousin David friend who happens to be Dj father who's gay. Throwing the party over there we had a blast and we went to my house late as fuck, drunk as fuck and Trey slept at my house right along with Missty who been sleeping at my house just like Mz. Trouble. Since it was a week left I kept myself busy having sex, scheming the low, even chilled with Ink one last time yet this visit the nigga brought his gun and showing it off. If it wasn't for GOD keeping eye on me that bullet would have hit me. It was so close to my left ear only an inch or less away from my and should have hit my ear if not scraping it instead, it went past my ear through my closet door and the wall behind my closet going straight outside leaving a ring noise and my ear hurting as the ringing was in my ears. Till this day I thank GOD for that and the number one reason why I hate guns. That same day I chilled Tev telling him and everyone I was leaving. Then there were the unexpected days as Neisha decided to lay with Mek-mek on the floor thinking she sleep of course till Mek-mek made a big deal of it causing a scene as I was in the other room with Dj in the process of fucking him yet the commotion outside made me see what was going on. Pissed at finding out what happen I was two seconds from flipping out on everybody and technically there was nothing I could do but if my cousin was to get in a fight with Mek-mek I wasn't doing shit and if there was jumping involved then me and my other two cousins was going to have to fight and I was ready yet nothing happen that night other than me wigging out before going back in my room. Neisha tried the shit again with Mz.Trouble coming home drunk and not realizing Neisha was in the bed with her holding her. She wasn't the only person who pissed me off since Missty too pissed me of having me have Toby pick her up from work thinking she was stranded not telling me she found a ride thanks to her soon to be husband having me worried sick about her and as soon as she came through my door I flipped out on her for having Toby waste gas to her not answering my phone calls. I even went to my court date down at the justice center going to housing court high off a pill yet I looked sober then a motherfucka. I sat there as I heard everyone case and when it was my turn I simply informed them I was moving out as he wanted me to yet the landlord was trying to make me pay the 225$ that Dai-dai never paid plus the rent for May and I wasn't having it so we set another court date little did the landlord know I was showing the judge pictures of the house complaining on how this house didn't have appliances to the lights having a shortage somewhere to the problem we had with the furnish not working to all the windows in the house were unable to open to the front hallway and bathroom doors having no handle causing me to be stuck in the bathroom way too many times and I was telling it all since I came to realize he was a slum landlord and wasn't getting a dime out my pocket. Since Dai-dai played me on the rent and didn't show up to court her mom deep fryer and hot plate was chalked along with the cooler she left over and since the gas was in her name I made sure the gas people ain't cut the service off since they never could get to the basement. All I was waiting on was Tez coming to take me from this hell whole. Up till the night Tez came in town I chilled with Mica to Tev one last time. Then the night came when Tez and Lex came through and after picking up Scooter us four plus Trey, Missty Neisha and David plus a few more including Mek-mek and Man we all chilled at my house drinking and geeking and playing cards as we listen to music yet I peeped Tez and what he was planning on doing and truth be told if I knew then what I know now I would of let Tez do what he do letting our past catch up with us. I realized Man was also drunk talking shit to Mek-mek yet I noticed Tez plotting to rob Man since he was flashing his money. See Tez planned was to rob and kill Man and we were on the road that night yet even though me and Meka wasn't talking I still considered her as my bestie at the time and me playing my roll I didn't want that to happen plus I didn't want to be on the run figuring the shit would be tied with me and Dai-dai being involved plus we couldn't leave any witness, so I wasn't digging that at all and after talking some since in him Tez dropped the topic and back to the party we went. That night everyone slept at my house and the next day we did the same shit after I went to papa Toby house to get some money to use for gas when I leave Cleveland. That night we went to Man house where Lil Mace had his b-day party at and after being there for two hours the party was back at my house with a different crowd having Marry and her baby daddy bring drinks along with Easy Mac and Roro and their kids. Coco and Mall even stopped by along with Sin and her company and we all including my people sat in a circle smoking and drinking and since this was my last weekend there I didn't care if the house was in good shape or not. I used the carpet as my personal astray and made sure I was to leave trash throughout the house along with leaving my bed and both t.v's in the house with some more unwanted clothes. After that night I was planning on leaving the next day making that night the last day of me staying on 116. Just as planed I packed all my personal items from tampons to shampoo to my jewelry to my high school diploma to my bible and grabbed the clothes I wanted and all my dishes including the shit Dai dai left and packed it all in Lex car and that day I chilled with Missty going back to that same house off Harvard where she spent her birthday at and after grilling and eating I left meeting up with Mz. Trouble who had also moved from my house to Juju house on Longwood. It was planned to be on the road that Monday morning after mother's day yet my whole family went to the zoo not telling me about it so I made other plans. Since this was going to be my last day I chilled with my sugar daddy during his lunch break sucking his little fella for the 3 to 5 minutes it took for him to shoot them blanks in exchanged for his weed and money. I also took a trip to Momma T house bringing both Chi-chi and Nasty Nate with me and the most funny shit happen after they met Pooder and his friend Cj who all made it known that all four of their daddy's were in jail all asking each other was they father in jail and once they realized they all had one thing in common (all their fathers were in jail) didn't stop till I left seeing Lisha, Nita and E-boo on the way back to Longwood. Since the fall out with Lisha it was more fuel to the fire saying I informed my mom on my dad having sex with Nita when she was 13 yet I set that record straight letting them know it was my godfather who told both my mom and I and after that incident I really didn't have too much to say to no one but Momma T. The remainder of that day I chilled at Juju house with Mz. Trouble, Trap, Dave and we smoked and talked shit as I was preparing to leave the next day headed to Michigan and as planned I was soon on the freeway early the next day smoking since I had the weed while Tez had the beer and playing music from my phone as we were on the freeway not knowing what I was walking into yet I was soon to find out. Going into Michigan I figured we was going to fill out the lease in see the house and Tez was to sell all his pills to a white boy yet when I got there things wasn't as I was told it was going to be. Driving to what people call it the Mexican territory we parked sat a house and I realized that Michigan cities were small. The downtown wasn't bigger then Cleveland State University campus. Cleveland felt like Texas against Ohio. Any who as we drove to a house Lex and I sat in the car for hours slowly getting hipped to the situation I was in. See the deal was to use the money that Tez was supposed to get and use that for one week of a hotel they wanted to stay at and on the second week I was to pay for a month at the hotel and as I stayed there Tez and Lex was to go to the blood bank receiving $200 week saving to get the house that he was telling me about and in the meantime Tez was supposed to be selling weed and my mom and Boogie pills for a little extra cash. As Lex was giving me the run down on everything I went from mad to angry as I thought about the lies Tez told me thinking that both of them had a job to us having a house to using me like my mom did for a stupid SSI check. Just then my mind had changed from staying in Michigan to going back to the C-Town and as bad as I didn't want to go back there I knew I had to if I want my own spot again do to the fact that I was now homeless just now in a different state with my brother who is also homeless fucking with his girlfriend and her hometown. That first night the three of us spent the night over some dude house that my brother met and that house was so too uncomfortable. He had cats and dogs everywhere giving off a bad odor yet the worst part was how the house looked. I know my great papa and my mother had a clutter house but this man house was clutter and nasty. I mean trash and dirty dishes were everywhere and a bitch didn't even want to take a piss but I did twice throughout my whole stay. What was creepy was this guy sleeping with a shotgun by the door while Lex and I slept in his son bedroom that says he don't get no pussy and his only son slept in his father bed while both Tez and the man house we were over slept in the living room. Waking up the next day I called Mz. Trouble and let her know what was going on and trying to figure a plan to get home hoping Toby would take the trip up here but never got an answer and since I put my 40$ in the gas on the way up here I was dead broke till next week and all I had was my food stamp card. After hanging up with her I called my mom who did nothing about the situation but instigate the beef between my brother and I that was starting up so I hung up with her and called papa Toby who I thought would save me but him too couldn't help for whatever reason he had and even told me I was fucked. Getting pissed off I was running out of options so I came up with a plan thanks to my mom about getting Tez and Lez go to the blood bank and using the money for gas to go back to Cleveland. The catch was that I lied telling them that my papa was going to pay them back waiting on my card so I changed Mz.Trouble contact name to my papa Toby name and texted her as if I was texting my papa Toby using that as proof that I wasn't laying my ass of on the low and the plan was as soon aa I brought the idea up to Tez it was a go but little did he know I was leaving them stuck in Cleveland while I disappeared doing my own thing. The second day was supposed to be ok yet Tez and I got into a heated argument about what I was spending my food stamp card on cooking it in my nu-wave oven in that man dirty ass house. I seen another side of him and realized I needed to hurry up in get out this situation even if I had to lay low for a while I needed my own spot asap. Instead of staying over there Lex left taking me to her mom house where I took a shower and chilled at her mom house for the next three days. After my first shower I masturbated wishing I could let someone fuck the anger and sadness out of me yet I wasn't close to home nor was I about to hoe it out in Grands Rapid Michigan so my finger was doable. Over the next two days I chilled with Lex meeting her mom and sister who is white and her dad side of the family cousins who were black and we rode around town showing off her small city. As she went to the blood bank I was pissed I couldn't donate blood since my blood count was at 11 so I was assed out. The plan was to wait till after the wedding and they will take me home which will solve the being homeless in another state part yet I didn't have a plan when I get to Cleveland. I just needed to crash at someone house till I got me a new spot to stay in. On my 5th day there I had to leave and go to a motel where Tez got a 4 day 3night stay at hotel and the day we was to leave was the day I was going back to Cleveland. Going to the motel I slept on the floor while Tez and Lez slept in a queen size bed going to bed that night. The next day as Lex was with her family for a dinner party Tez and I chilled at the hotel smoking, drinking beer and eating some roast chicken that taste like Boston Market roast chicken and that night all three of us slept in the bed as I took a six hour nap waking up late that night. Since it was two days left I was too pumped to go back home I just needed one more day of this shit. The next day as Lex went to her aunty wedding Tez left me in the house by myself with 2 blunts and some beer for me to drink. That day was peaceful as fuck as I watched the movie underworld 2x masturbated all in the bed as I thought about me leaving going home tomorrow. Going to bed that night I noticed Lex coming in asking where my brother was yet since neither of us knew where he was at she left looking for him. That night they didn't come back and I didn't care as long as they were here before check out time but as the next day came about neither of them showed up and since both Tez and Lex didn't have a phone I couldn't contact them nor the minute phone Scooter gave to Tez. Calling Lex mom she was no help and neither was mines so I began crying wondering what went wrong. I even began to pray to God something I didn't do in a long time crying and letting GOD know how hurt I was even though he knew it already. Just as I thought things wouldn't be worse it did. Finally opening the door I seen both Tez and Lex walk in the house yet the news he gave me I didn't expect. Since I did a late checkout I had to leave by 1p.m and it was 15minutes away. Telling me the news I was informed about the situation I was told that Tez crashed the car over an argument with Lex and instead of dropping the topic Tez tried to kill both him and her crashing into a light pole leaving the car there. I instantly started to cry again since now all my stuff was gone and I was still homeless and without a way to Cleveland. Since it was time to leave I asked Tez what we were going to do and he told me to find my own way to Cleveland and he has nowhere to take me so they were getting ready to drop me off the greyhound station. Calling Meka who I haven't talked to since the fall out I called begging her to save me and give me a ticket. She claimed she could helped yet we was to drive all the way to Detroit Michigan to the Walmart yet Lex mom wasn't doing the ride so I was helpless. At that very last moment God came through like a thief at night and used Cece to pay for my ticket and by the time Tez left me at the station saying "I don't have nowhere for you to go, so u going to have to stay here till someone pay for a ticket" and left and that same time God saved me yet again. This time he used Cece the same girl I beat up just last year to pay for my ticket and after Tez dropped me at the greyhound station I had 2 in a half hours left till the next greyhound bus leaving Cleveland and even after everything and I do mean everything from my bible to my jewelry to all my clothes to all my dishes to my personal things were all in the trunk besides my purse my two covers, the white load I left with Lex mom to and pillows and three outfits were at the hotel and as I grabbed the little things that I did have left I only took my three outfits I had left wearing one out the outfits packing the two other outfits and one literally only had one bra and three thongs to work with yet getting back to Cleveland was the main thing. Since I stole 5$ from Lex and her mom giving me 5$ I had enough to buy a dime bag and smoke it. I even had to leave my covers and pillows with Lex as I was at the station by myself. During the visit some dude in a wheelchair got the nerve to ask me would I keep him company after reading a scripture from the bible. At that moment I thought about saying fuck my life, leave with this strangers and find my own way in Michigan living the streets just like Tez yet there was that other side saying u can get through this, I don't know how but you will so instead of leaving with the stranger I patiently waited for my bus to departure from the greyhound. Only six hours did it take me to get back to Cleveland coming in town at 1:20 am to Uncle Curtis picking me up dropping me off to Juju house in Longwood where Mz. Trouble and Toby was at. The next few days I stayed over Juju house chilling with Juju, Mz. Trouble staying in the house. Before the week was over I went Cece over someone's house where we spent the night at and the next day a bitch went to Wal-Mart in the Steelyards and stole five pair of pants and a few tank tops and afterwards I met up with Mz. trouble and we all went over BigB house off Eddy road where I spent two days there and since I had a few food stamps left I went to Save-a-lot where I bought a little food such as a pack of noodles, French fries and tater tots with pizza rolls and a loft of bread and other little stuff. Leaving the food there I chilled with Mz trouble, Toby and his lee rd. friends from Trap, Dre to littleD and Chinney including having Mek-mek and Cece joined the party and we all went to the creek where we got drunk at and smoked cracking jokes. The plan was to move in with either with BigB or Juju yet I was undecided so I went with the flow and wherever Mz. Trouble went I went with her. I felt like we were both homeless together so let's be in the homeless stage together. Finally coming up with a plan I was going to North folk Vagina leaving the 1st weekend of June and the only person that knew I was leaving was papa Toby. The plan was to stay with Meka and her husband for two months causing me to stack up and I was finding my own spot and I needed it bad yet before I left I was in another pointless fight now that I think about it. Two days before I left as I was chilling over Juju house with her cousin Toby, Mek-mek and Mz. Trouble and long story short BigB became the big elephant in the room as I found out she lied to me about the situation between Mek-mek and BigB then for BigB leaving Mz. Trouble outside in her car with Chi-chi ignoring their calls as they were outside her house waiting to get in and instead of letting them in she slept in Toby truck and after Mek-mek checked BigB she let it be known that she was going to fight her and I was ready if I had to fight. After she hung up on her we went two cars deep to BigB house planning to fight her yet I didn't have a reason to fight her yet but when I got there to her house and I found out she ate my food I left there two days ago I decided to start the fight by throwing the first punch fighting from the bathroom to her bedroom punching her repeatedly and a bitch was whipping her ass then out of nowhere BigB grabbed a radio attempting to hit me with it missing the first time but as she did it the second time it hit me in the head and that's when Mz. Trouble jumped in at hitting her and grabbing the radio then as the radio was gone BigB decided to bite me as both Mz. Trouble and I was jumping on her and out of nowhere Mek-mek jumped in for a second as we all attacked her. I even decided to bite BigB back in the stomach right before the two guys that were there watching the fight finally decided to break up the fight and as the fight was broken up we all ran out her house but not before destroying the kitchen as we made our exit around the corner to Mz. Trouble friend house where I cleaned my bite mark I still got on my left arm and we all talked about the fight yet little did anyone know I was leaving in two days. Waking up the next day I had to go to my second court date yet before I did that Juju had me grab all my stuff since she was on her way to see her baby daddy in jail and by the time I was to come back she wasn't going to be there so since I had weed on me I grabbed my bag of clothes and left out headed to Man house to drop my stuff off. Going back downtown I just missed my court date by five minutes and I was pissed that I wasn't able to show up so who knows what was said and I was mad I couldn't tell my case knowing I was going to complain my ass off and had a good chance to win this case yet I never had a chance to. After asking around I couldn't change my court date I left heated as fuck and to make me more upset riding the bus I past Juju house I noticed she was still there and after getting off the bus to her house I noticed nether her or Nasty Nate was dress meaning she was lying about her being gone by the time I went to court. Since I left a few things at her house, I took them and went back over Man house where I met up with Marry and we got to drinking and rolling up blunts for the 17hour trip I was taking to North folk and in the meantime after drinking with Marry I had her drop me off back over Man house where I smoked with Lil Mace while waiting on my papa Toby to pick me up that night and as planned he did taking me to Walmart to get a few items and I went to his house where I spent the night watching my ten outfits I managed to have after receiving two too big outfits from BigB. Waking up that morning a 5a.m I had papa Toby drop me off at the greyhound station and running late I was finally on the bus on my way down south drinking and listening to music and a bitch was feeling herself thinking her problems were now gone. I site seen different cities and state from Baltimore which seem like a nice place to other cities as we went toward Vania passing West Vania and when we took breaks a bitch smoked a blunt and a mild both rest stops we had. Soon as I pulled up in the station did Meka dumb ass informed me that she moved from North Folk to Chicago and what pissed me off was that Lil Mace said she moved and not listening I was now in another different state by myself. Pissed the fuck off and too embarrassed to tell my papa Toby I went to call my mom and Uncle Spanky since he stayed in Charleston West Virginal yet neither one of them could help and after talking to Meka I still was out of luck and neither did she pay my way nor apologize for having me go the opposite way. If that was the case I would of just left grands rapid to Chicago since they were literally underneath each other so I decided to get a ticket yet again for the third time and head back to Cleveland undecided on what I was going to do. Having papa Toby pay my ticket online I had to wait 6hours for the next bus and during the meantime I talked to Micca letting her in on my situation and it was planned for me to move in with her for the remainder of the month yet I wasn't letting no one know that I was coming back to Cleveland instead I had everyone besides my mom, papa Toby and Micca and Man think I was in Chicago with Meka. As I toured Virginia I smoked and got me something to eat looking at different landmarks before going back to the station where the bus was coming late night and as soon as it came I was on there, patiently waiting on my return to Cleveland but not before passing the scary tunnel underneath the water to the mountains that consist of trees with no lights in sight so the darkness plus the image made it look scary as fuck but I closed my eyes played my music and was sipping on the Bacardi I had mixed with strawberry kiwi juice. During the breaks I smoked outside getting geeked and was soon on my way to Cleveland and as soon as I made it closed to Cleveland I let Micca know I was close and once I got to town I met Micca on 40th in Community College Drive where she gave me her key and I gave her some money to get some bud and I headed straight to her house where I masturbated on her bed and afterwards took a long hot shower and drank the rest of my liquor waiting for Micca to slide through until then I caught up on some sleep laying in her bed till she got there and when she got there I got high spending the first night at her house. Staying with her was ok for the most part and since I was laying low everywhere she went I went. I even let Tev and my sugar daddy know that I was back in town and I used my sugar daddy for the usual weed and money he gave me in and return we either fucked, gave him a blow job or on this occasion I acted like I was on my period so he wouldn't touch me. I stayed going to her mom house to sitting in her house all day with the ac smoking and some days her uncle came through smoking. Since she had no t.v we stayed listening to music playing cards and on the days her uncle came through we watched movies on his t.v that he brought over every time and since everything was in one room we literally sat there in that one room. That whole month I didn't talk to anyone and far as boys wise go I chilled with Tev and my sugar daddy minus the times I went over Man house to get some bud. One time going over Man house I ran into Mz.Phoo and "Kid" gf at the time and didn't notice it was her till Man said something about it I even used Man house to meet my sugar daddy at just to get some more money and weed and I spent his money on more weed so I'll be cool the whole month of June as long as I was to stay high and have food and take a shower I was cool. Going over Man house I also found out that him and his families were going through things their self. Right before I left to go to Michigan did Man come to my house after getting out of jail. Telling the story behind it I found out that Shorty who is a friend I met through Meka had set Man up using her brother to buy some weed form him not knowing Shorty was wired plus they were in a undercover cop car and after the exchanged the police made it seem like Shorty was going to jail yet that next day the police came through Man house and all he had time for was to throw his best friend Deuce who died over a year ago and now wished I would of fucked his cute ass too but anyway not before Big Mace who is "Kid", J and Lil Mace father(and yes I did fuck all three brothers but only fuck with one of them but not how he think I fucks with him) ran through the house grabbing certain shit and not even five minutes later was Man attacked by police officers and going to jail. While I was in Michigan both Big Mace and his sister San who is Man mom were both arrested on the account off selling drugs to being on PCP which they are still on today while Man was out on bail holding down the house. The deal was to pay Micca 25$ rent and as long as we kept food in the fridge and I kept bud everything should have been cool and it was for the most part. We went from inviting different friends over and I fucked one of my brother friends Lj in Micca bathroom throwing it back to meeting a bud man two doors down from her apartment who she fucked that night while I fucked his brother. That whole night we fucked all through that house after I gave the bud man brother a quickie in their mom bed and what stopped us was his mom coming home and after seeing us walk out her room I didn't want to stay there so we all went back to Micca house where I went from the floor to the bed fucking him in different positions and even though his dick wasn't as big as I wanted it to be I did feel good and he kept us high smoking blunt after blunt as the hours of the next day rolled in and since this was a studio there was no privacy yet no one cared since sex was in the air. Somedays I would go over

Micca mom house but after getting the vibe that none of her sisters but the youngest and older one liked me I had that fuck you attitude and even though I gave my respect it was known to two sisters that I didn't like them as much as they didn't like me and they were so petty that they didn't want me playing with their kids so I barely went there and each time I did I only spoke to Micca mom and her two sisters who seemed to like me and kept it moving. One day I even had my dad slide through with an uncle of mines and after cooking for us we all ate got high and played spades and they beat us. Other days I stayed in the house either by myself or with Micca sometimes bringing her uncle who I was teasing knowing he found me attractive. The security guard at her building even had a thing for me yet I wasn't fucking him yet. Then we had the dumbest day from just being outside all day if not taking her to the blood bank on the west side to us hoping in a car with a dude Micca just met and since we ain't have shit to do and left with them as we went to his apartment with his friend. Going over there we started drinking and geeking and things were cool till they asked me to cook something to eat. It wasn't what he said it was how he said it yet I didn't say anything. Looking in the kitchen I came up with the idea to cook some steak sandwiches yet I wasn't about to do it myself. Asking the friend to help he acted like he didn't know what he was doing so I gave him a simple solution to spread the sandwich spread on the bread his dumbass replied "I don't know how to do that" and as soon as he said that I stopped what I was doing in headed in the bathroom to use my phone. Getting interrupted Micca told me that we was leaving and had to catch the bus back to her house since the guys wanted to fuck and since we wasn't fucking them they wasn't dropping us off back home so I got off the phone, grabbed my stuff and out the door we went. Finding out I was on Euclid I used my free RTA bus card and got us home since Micca was throwing up outside I rushed going home chilling the rest of the night in the a.c. Our days were so random we went from being in the house to meeting back up with my friend Moe who is Dai-dai 1st lover and after linking back up with him since he just got out of jail I went with him to sell 2oz of bud to Man meeting him and "Kid" at Edgewater lake where we did the exchanged leaving with Man going back to Micca house where we chilled just the four of us before the two boys left. As the ending of June came around I started to get aggravated with Micca and her ways. She went from being cool to catching attitudes and her house was starting to bore me sitting in one room with nothing to do and on the days she left me stuck in the house was getting to me so I took a two day vocation over Man house seeing Tev during the time. I was supposed to stay three days but on the second night of me being there not only did Man tell me that San didn't want me here but he got mad and told everyone to leave out his house after being gone with his baby mama aka (loose lips) driving San car. By the time we came back he went off on everybody including me and it was known he didn't want anyone at his house so I left. I figured he was mad that his mom and Uncle was in Jail yet Mz. Trouble and I was in our own situation being homeless plus Trap just got shot 2x in the back I knew everyone was going through something of their own so I respected that and left till my anger calmed down from being mad at Man. Giving a few days I went back over Man house running into Mz. Trouble so I had to act like I just came back in town and we all chilled over Man house that night. Leaving the next day I took Chi-chi with me as we went back over Micca house and stayed in the house. Little did anyone know the last visit to Man house I talked to him knowing the situation he was in and took him up on his offer on staying with him $200 a month. Figuring I need a place to stay and didn't want to stay over Micca house the next month I took him up on his offer but not before asking my family for help. My mom never gave me an answer and papa Toby told me I couldn't stay with him because of his wife, My dad wasn't no help since he was staying with people and I never messed with any of my mom side of the family especially aunty Moochie who act like she wasn't at home the last visit I came over there to tell her about my situation and from what I was told Spanky wasn't opening up his house to me and hearing Tez, Cash and Scooter feedback I shouldn't want to go down there so I had no options since I was will been in the streets for two years now and I ain't even know it so I settled with staying with Man and his house and I planned to keep myself busy hanging with his neighborhood friends. I was just waiting till my 30 days were up and since July1st was a day away I only had five days to make my move yet Micca gave me three days to make it happen. Just as the first hit I had Mz. Trouble take me to Walmart where I got two bras and two packs of panties plus two packs of socks and bought five short set outfits and brought it back to Micca house and after getting a quarter I was cool. Going over my papa Toby house the next day he let me wash my one load of clothes while I gave Man the 150$ and I chilled with Mz. Trouble over her aunty house while she cheated on Toby with Al-be and that night I went back to Micca house bringing Chi-chi with me and we stayed there that whole night. As soon as chi-chi was sleep I called old dude who is brothers of the bud Man and I fucked him one last time in Micca bed going to bed happy yet when I woke up I woke up to drama as usual. Waking up to Micca yelling about who was in her house I ignored her ever since she sent me a text asking was Chi-chi still with me the day before. After her clothes were dropped off she kept asking me who was in her house and why was Chi-chi still here. Then what flipped me out was the bitch had the nerve to kick me out as if I wasn't planning on leaving a day later so I called Mz. Trouble and long story short after going back in fourth of us putting each other shit in and out the hallway I was greeted with the management lady and we all waited for Mz. Trouble to come through same time Mica was accusing me or my company of stealing her sim-card from her old phone she had that some stranger she fucked after a day of meeting him and still saying I had someone in her house. I figured the security guard downstairs must have told her something for her to think I had people in her house. As soon as Toby and the crew came we all grabbed my stuff and I left with my shit packed up already and after dropping it off at Man house and going up the street to Woodhill Park where Toby I and Mz trouble got geeked and Mek-mek and Roro was there as well. I also found the SIM card that was on her floor and after being outside Toby threw in in the air. See the plan was for me to move with Man for a while and by September I should have me a spot and since it was only July I figured I had no choice but to roll with it by keeping myself busy with the different people from Man hood. For starters I spent Mz. Trouble b-day at Man house and since I found some weed sitting around we smoked that shit up in Toby truck chilling in Man backyard. Some days I will chill with Man and his friends from the hood including Nitty and Cliff to chilling with Shorty since her baby daddy friends stopped fucking with her and other days I chilled with Tev but most days I was with Mz. Trouble and Toby chilling with his Lee RD clique going places from the creek to the lake getting drunk and geeking on the low. See staying at Man house was something else. My problem was the dirtiness. I mean roaches were everywhere one time popping on Mz. Trouble and her freaking out made me freak out and we all slept in Toby truck that night. That wasn't the only problem just like in 2010 Man house stayed dirty everywhere you went. The fridge microwave and oven were too filthy even dead roaches was stuck in the microwave and their bathroom was a mess that I never took a shower there instead them hoe baths came in handy. Since I stayed out and about I barely stayed in the house besides the day I chilled with Man baby mama who went to the same elementary school and other time I was in the house was to go to bed if I wasn't there already so we would play the catching up process. Since I still seen my sugar daddy I will have him meet me at Man house not letting him know my situation yet this day he came was funny to everyone but Tev. As usual he was meeting after he got off so after riding with Toby and Mz. Trouble we picked up Mek-mek who wanted to go over Man house to check Man baby mama about how she talked to Mek-mek and I had my agenda. Getting out the truck wearing black and pink stripe tank top with some black bootie shorts with black flip flops I took from Micca and wore some boy shorts underneath and as soon as I hit the corner I heard Tev yell "damn" through the window and I knew he was staring at my ass, legs and thighs and I was low-key loving the attention little did he know I was wearing it to tease someone else. As soon as we got in the house Mek-mek went straight upstairs to confront Man baby mama about her aptitude yet no one fault so the beef was squashed and my eyes but that wasn't the funny part. At first it was only Man, his baby mama, Toby Mz. Trouble Chi-chi and myself till Tev invited his self over like he usually did yet the last time they seen each other they were about to fight. Not only that Tev was talking shit bout Toby to me saying he would of beat Toby ass which everyone doubted that and I went back and told Mz. Trouble only for her to tell Toby. Since we were all in the living room Toby tried to bring the convo up between Tev and me about Toby yet Man ignorant ass trying to keep peace kept cutting on the vacuum so no one could hear each other talk. Thank goodness my phone ringed and it was my sugar daddy telling me he will be there and five minutes and was happy as hell. As soon as he was outside I hopped up leaving without anyone noticing yet when I got up Man let it be known that I was about to leave with my sugar daddy and as those words came out his mouth Tev almost called me a hoe for the second time saying "so she is a h" even though he never said the word I felt he still called me one so as I hopped in my sugar daddy black truck I left to suck his little fella for the usual three to five minutes letting him fuck me in his wife bed and even took me a tour of his house where from the dinning rom and basement was packed with weed that he was growing throughout his house. I made sure to spend some time with Tev kissing him and two days later not brushing my teeth I kissed his ass sticking each every inch of my tongue down his throat. As a few days past I kept myself busy either kicking it with Shorty to Tev to Man and his friends to Mz. Trouble and the same group and things were cool. I even ran back into Mr. Juju who I slowly got hipped that he was fucking with Juicy J and had two babies by her yet he was trying to fuck me and since I had left my wallet with Mek-mek at her house I had no choice but to hop in the car with him to avoid the long walk I was about to take and after he took me to pick up my stuff I let him hit and that nigga still felt good ass I was giving him my famous favorite back shots position same time he saying shit in my ear slapping my ass and I enjoyed it and afterwards I went about my day back over Man hood where I spent the remainder of that day getting high with Shorty. Since I was having a good time I decided to stay another month even though I didn't want to yet do to the drama that was going on the decision I made next was easy. For starters I was told a rumor about me fucking a guy on the couch the same night Mz. Trouble stayed over and the same night Cliff tried to fuck me yet I only fucked Tev and my sugar daddy that month yet since she had a problem with me so I had a problem with her as well. As the end of July came back I should have expect what was coming. Taking Man to his court date I sat there as the trial was for all three San, Big Mace and Man I watched as both San and Big Mace were finishing a sentence and when it was Man turn I set and listened to the judge as they sentence him to six months and as I watched him walk away I cried thinking about both our situations we were in. Not only was I now the only person who would be in the house but me actually missing Man I don't know what I was going to do since all four Toby, Mz. Trouble Man and myself bond became stronger as this year went by. Going back to his house that night Man baby mama packed her shit and left but not till she ran her mouth telling DeMan who told the whole hood that Man was locked up meaning everyone knew the house would be empty which scared me the first night of me staying there thinking someone was going to break in the house. That whole night I talked to Tev just so I want feel alone and masturbated all in San bed and soon as the morning it I got up, took my hoe bath and went straight to Shorty house where I spent the day getting high as usual. The next day San had Booty one of Big Mace baby mama came to move in with her son Shawn who I fucked in the den that she ain't know. Moving in with her there was a problem still. One night she locked the door knowing I was on the porch talking to Mz. Trouble after leaving the house since Booty acted like she didn't want no one in the house and after that incident I knew I was going to move I don't know where yet though lucky for me I ran into Shar meeting a guy name Los and after talking to her I came to the solution to move out Man house to Shar house staying the month of August at her house and I would be looking for a house that month. As soon as August 1st hit I was out the house and moved to Shar house where I waited in the hallway of her door for two hours masturbating as the time went by till Shar finally came through. Going into her house I could tell she just moved in. All she had was two covers a chair and a storage container. The deal was to pay $200 to $150 but since her rent was only 25 dollars we came to a conclusion to pay her $80 yet I was only paying her ass $50. That night of me being there I took a long hot shower and went to bed on the floor since she ain't have no bed. I was comfortable though that the house was clean plus a.c and I could take a shower so as long as I kept food in the house, weed in our system and taking her to the blood bank

I was cool and figured she should feel the same way as the 1st week went by. She even went with me to papa Toby house to get high with my dad and me pick up some money from my papa Toby since he been my payee for the last three months to going with her to her boyfriend house on 93rd. Often I was there by myself if not with Mz. Trouble all day smoking my life away. Since Man was now in jail with his family I never went back over there and was only cool with a few people from Mountview so I only chilled with Shorty having her meet Mz. Trouble and the one thing they had in common was the fact that they both fuck with Al-be who was fucking them the same month. As the first week went by things were cool but that Saturday after the 1st week I went downtown to Tower city with Mz. Trouble and Chi-chi and that day I ain't see coming but I was waiting for that day. Going into Tower city I ran into my cousin who happens to be Mz. Trouble cousin which was strange to me but who cares. The same spot I ran into Nikki and Shar and all the stuff Nikki was talking on Facebook I meant what I said about fighting her when I see her since she was talking stuff five months ago so as planned I followed her to the bathroom where we ran into BigB and what was crazy is that all five of us Shar, Nikki, BigB, Mz. Trouble and I all were cool since we all went to Hope High yet things changed as the school closed and no one really fucked with no one. After leaving the bathroom I followed her outside where the fight began across the street from the Renaissance hotel downtown and after Nikki threw the rest of her caramel frappe' the fight began as punches were being thrown back and forth till we were in a lock position and stayed that was till stand byers separated us and after a little more arguing I followed Shar in Nikki to the Renascence and I followed her leaving both Mz. Trouble and Chi-chi outside with my purse and phone. Going into the restroom the look on Nikki face was priceless and I knew she was mad about her face and after noticing me standing there the fight began again punching each other all across the bathroom until we heard a door open up which made us stop and go into the stalls. As soon as they left out the bathroom the fight began again fighting across the floor again almost biting her ear to smashing her face to the mirror trying to break it yet we heard the door again and stopped the fight again and I ran to the handicap person stall while Shar and Nikki was elsewhere and as soon as the second group left the fight started we fault again this time Nikki grabbed me by the shirt swinging my body and a circle till I fell on the marble floor. Making an attempt to stand over me fighting I squirmed from underneath her swinging and slowly but surely she repeated the same thing and I got my ass right back up and we literally fault till we were tired and out of breath and the whole time Shar watched the whole thing. After the fight I realized my arm was sore just like the pain I felt when I fought Kandi two years ago. Not paying attention I exited the hotel finding Mz. Trouble with my purse and after drinking some pop thinking I was dehydrated the vomit started to come out of nowhere and it wouldn't stop so a staff member called EMS shipping me to Metro where I was getting treated for the vomiting problem I develop March25,2011. Meanwhile I complained to the nurse that my arm was sore and felt strange and after the x-ray I was told that my shoulder was dislocated and that it needed to get popped back in place. All I remember is getting a mask on my face as the doctor told me to countdown from 50 yet I only made it to 46 and I was knocked out. All I remember was waking up saying woeeeeeee" as my vision was blurry and I was dizzy then lights out again and the next time I woke up I was in a sling and waiting on papa Toby to pick me up dropping me back off at Shar house where I went to sleep. The next day I chilled with Shar talking about the fight as we smoked by the pound by her house and I spent the next two days at her house meeting a guy name D'nell which I used him for his money and weed that he sold. I even met a cute light skin guy I call ATL since that's what he's from and ended up fucking both of them in Shar house since I was either by myself in her house and both wanted their dicks sucked yet it wasn't happening. Other days, I wasn't at Shar house I chilled with Mz Trouble having her roll up blunts for me taking it back to Shar house smoking it by myself most of the time. I even took Shar to the Woodhill festival where I met up with Shorty and even ran into a few people from my 6th grade teacher Ms.J to the bud men that stayed in Micca building and I enjoyed myself that day. I also heard a family reunion was coming and I didn't want to go yet when I found out that Tez and his new gf came in town the both of them plus my mom and other two siblings went to the water park with my uncle Cash. What pissed me off is no one asked me did I want to go nor did anyone on that side or my dad side showed me that they didn't give a fuck about me or being in the streets so I felt completely alone for the 1st time yet since the reunion was coming I was making sure I spend the rest of my money that I was using as spending money and was going to turn with the fam on my mother mom side of the family plus I assumed no one from my family from both my uncles and aunty wasn't coming and I just knew my mom wasn't going to be there. What's crazy is Tez had me waiting on him to pick me up from Shar house yet he never came and I was too pissed. As the 3rd week of me staying there I went from looking at houses to stealing me an outfit from the store Forman Mills after waking up the wrong way causing my left shoulder to slowly pop out of place feeling the discomfort in my arm. For the grace of GOD me messing with my shoulder in a circle motion I felt the pain disappear as I went to finally get up. After talking to both papa Toby and Missty we decided to go to the reunion together. As the day of the reunion came about I went on 105 to get my hair done by a friend of Shorty who I peeped out was cold on the hair side and I gave her a first shot of doing my hair including putting on my lashes and after I changed in her bathroom I was ready to meet up with Missty and party and as planned my papa Toby took us to the reunion and the smoking session began. Seeing a few faces and seeing some I stopped seeing since my granny death and others I didn't know. To my surprise I seen Spanky coming up with his family and seeing his son Jr. for the 1st time he looked just like Spanky and my #1 papa. After introducing him to papa Toby I seen my #1 papa and Cash coming up and since I was mad at Cash for not picking me up with Tez I ain't say nothing to him but spoke to his dad. Then out of nowhere I seen my mom and two siblings come thru and since I haven't seen them in months. I was happy to see them yet me and my mom didn't speak and I was fine with that. Leaving with Spanky we went to join my other cousins who like getting high and we smoked out our lungs sipping on whatever was in my drink and just as the mood was right Tez came through with three of his friends and the party in the back just began. As the elders were in the front in the pavilion all the smokers were in the parking lot having a party of our on. As I was geeked I noticed everyone flashing clothes, cars from old school to hummers and I was getting pissed off. I notice people ain't give a fuck bout they whole family and realize we are not as closed as we would have been if my granny was still alive. What pissed me of is no one really knew what I was going through and seeing how self-center my family was they weren't going to give a fuck about me and I let it be known starting with going off on Cash till saying fuck you to Moochie fake ass and after Spanky calmed me down I went back to the smoking session. In my head it felt like my granny was there since everyone else but her was there and I was salty that she wasn't here and even madder that if she was alive we would have had the time of our lives since she was known to throw parties just like my mom do. I even wanted to tell on everyone letting my granny know how everyone was acting after her death yet she was gone and wasn't coming back and that itself was enough pain to last a lifetime. As the party went on a list was being past to have everyone info yet I never filled it out nor did I eat yet I didn't care I was getting under the influence with the world most fakest family I know till the party ended and everyone was going their separate ways yet since both Tez and Spanky were staying an extra day instead of leaving with papa Toby I left with Spanky going to a hotel where the group I was with drunk a little bit and smoke Michigan and West Vagina weed till we all fell asleep but I was unaware of what I was waking up to. GOD and his many mysterious ways had came at an unexpected time and at the last minute yet, it was right on time. Waking up that morning I was in a sad mood knowing everyone was going to their regular happy lives being with other love one yet I was stuck by myself and was slowly going back to Shar house for another week in a half to three weeks depending on how soon I can find a house yet GOD had another plan. Checking my voicemail I was left a message from my papa Toby telling me that my money came through and I had 13 hundred to work with and as soon as I heard the news I thanked GOD for his many, many blessings and my spirit changed from being sad to being and after I called papa Toby back I let him know that I will get in touch with him once I figured out what I was going to do with the money. Too happy I only told Spanky and soon as they left the hotel I got dropped off at Shar house after seeing Mrs. Ann and as usual I had to wait on her to come home in let me in. That whole day Monday I was looking in the newspaper looking for any house that was available and that Wednesday I seen a spot on west 44th off Clark and after seeing it my thirsty ass paid the $750 the next day getting my keys that Thursday and Friday I ordered me a bed having it delivered in an hour to my house in the meantime I went to Family dollar on west 25th and walked my ass to my new house I wouldn't be sharing with no one and I cleaned that house bleaching everything in by the time I was done my bed was delivered and I locked my house up going back to Shar house. Still not telling no one I gave Shar $50 saying she was getting her other $30 soon yet I wasn't planning on giving it to her. I got the concept of people taking advantage of a person regardless rather they were in a fucked up position or not. People only gave a fuck about me when it's benefiting them not caring what bridges they were burning on the way. That Saturday I decided to get my hair done by Shorty friend only this time the visit was different. Meeting up with Shorty we went to the hair store where I bought my hair and lashes and watched the look on Shorty face as I bought what I needed while she couldn't because she didn't have no money and after meeting her friend on 93rd in Yale she started on my hair as the four people in the house including me started to get high while my hair was getting done. Things were cool till I went to the restroom to get me a front bang yet as I was getting my hair flat ironed Shorty friend warned me about grabbing my purse and just as I was told I moved my purse from one room to the next hanging it behind the door in the room I had my three blunts rolled up. Seconds later Shorty came in the bathroom complementing my hair at the same time I heard movement outside the bathroom and whatever was going on out there I heard someone run down the stairs and seconds later a group of niggas came upstairs headed to the room my stuff was in and as soon as they were in the room I followed grabbing my purse but as I looked in it expecting $86 yet as bad as I wanted my eyes to deceive me it didn't work and instead of the $86 I was left with 6$ and since I discovered this before the group of guys came it was only the four of us yet since both me and Shorty friend were in the bathroom it left two people that could of done it and thinking Shorty was my friend I blame fuck boy who just so happened was fucking both Shorty and her friend back in the day. Accusing him I checked his ass and after searching his pockets I came up empty handed. Then to make things worse the three blunts I had on the table were now gone and it was obvious that the group of guys that came through took it so my whole day felt fucked up. Using the last $6 I bought another sack, a mild was given to me and as Shorty, her friend and I minus the fuck guy I let them both in on that I will find out who did it and when I do I'm coming for revenge since I was a vengeful person. That night my gut was telling me Shorty had something to do with it and going over her house the next day it was strange how she got money and lashes to and by the time I got there her hair was done yet I never said nothing. Going back to Shar house that night I was going to leave out on the first yet only after being there the 2nd day did I leave. Waking up that morning Shar and I chilled with ATL smoking some bud he gave us when D'Nell popped up as usual pissing me off since no one invited him so I rudely ignored him till Shar was pissed that he was still knocking at her door after 15minutes passed. Finally opening the door he rudely pushed the door open causing it to hit me and I flipped. Assuming he was going to hit me I began punching him from the kitchen back to the hallway where a neighbor saw the commotion and threatened to call the police as I was throwing blows repeatedly with my one hand till he was safe away from her door and figuring they was going to call the police I went in Shar house and D'Nell went wherever he went. That day I decided to let that be my last day staying in her building and after calling papa Toby I packed my shit lying telling Shar I was just washing yet I wasn't planning on coming back. Going over papa Toby house I spent two days there going shopping for the house since I was working with 600$ now and I got me a table to a comfort bed set to dishes and pot and pans and dropped it all at my house. Going with papa Toby I went over Momma T house where Lisha dropped the beef of whatever we had by showing me an award of some sort and that day I gave her a 2nd chance yet I was playing it cool since Lisha pulled that stunt kicking me out the projects she no longer lived in thanks to her friend getting busted selling drugs causing Lisha to move yet she had another place but that didn't last before she was back at her mom house on 30th and I felt like that what she got for kicking me out. It was also said that I went and told my mom what my dad did to Nita which was a lie and that started the distance relationship but by the end of the day she was doing my kinky twist that Friday of Labor day weekend. That weekend I bought me two outfits and went from one party to the next stating with an all-white party for my dad siblings at a bar Coventry and I had a blast. Going with my dad I went to one of his girl house and we drunk and got geeked more till I went to sleep and the next day it was a party at my papa Toby house and after spending a night I went to my house where I dropped some more stuff off. Waiting on the lights and gas to come on I spent one week over Momma T house till the gas was on yet I missed my first appointment I had to wait till the 12th of September to get my gas on yet that whole day was odd. For starters the gas man walked in on me brushing my teeth in the bathroom wearing some boy shorts yet I wasn't offended or ashamed plus he liked what he saw by the look on his face and since he was a cute mixed dude I liked him too plus I like to talk shit and today was one of those days. I let him have a good view of my ass to letting him see my tongue ring knowing guys like that and talking shit began. Long story short he was willing to pay yet I thought he was bluffing till he came back with 20s in his hand and made me speechless and guess what.......I didn't even fuck him yet I gave him my # and till this day I regret not fucking him. Before he left I got a call from Shorty asking me to use my bus card to go to the steelyard to hit up a couple spots yet the only thing that was going on in my head was to rob Shorty and I let Lisha in on the plan and told her to stay by the phone. Rushing to Shorty house it took me over an hour but I made it just in time for her to go to the bank in the plaza and watched her take $140 then goes to the atm machine to withdraw $60 then had the nerve to find $20 and adding it up it was a total of $220 and I was planning on stealing it all right there outside but I decided to wait to till I got in her house. Safely in her house I waited as the opportunity presented itself and as soon as she walked in the bathroom I took her money and after five minutes I came up with a lame excuse to leave and as soon as I was outside I let Lisha know what I did and I met her on 30th, bought a half oz. of weed and smoked with her and her godmother turning my phone off. Even though I did what I did the drama still didn't end there. After having my phone turned off, I turned it back up and seen all the miss calls from Tev to Man baby mama to Lil Mace which was the only person I replied to and after texting back and forth I had him meet me at Tri-c thinking he was with "Kid" yet as I was walking out the projects I felt this bad gut feeling about something and another words GOD was telling me something that I didn't understand till I seen lil Mace walking with the same friend I seen earlier when I was with Shorty and right then in there I knew it was a set up and I went back in the projects letting Lisha know what was going on and the plan was to stay put since no one knew where I was at yet Lisha god brother told them where I was at the drama started. Right then I knew I had to fight and I was war ready yet I was pissed that I text lil Mace thinking he was on my side not knowing he was setting me up. At first I went to the door acting like I didn't know what was going on yet things got out of hand when Pete who is Shorty fuck boy who she was cheating on her baby daddy bud man was standing in front of Lisha trying to pull me out the door by grabbing my jeans pants pocket yet since Lisha was in front of me he couldn't pull me through the door thanks to Lisha pushing him out the door. By then I thought I had to fight yet I wasn't getting jumped since Pete made it known he had beef with me. Since Shorty wasn't a match for me I wasn't bothered nor threatened by her since I knew I could beat her ass I was worried about what Pete was on knowing he had nothing to do with the situation and the arguing began. I was getting heated that I told Shorty remembering the convo I had with Shorty and her friend about me getting her back for what she and fuck boy did and after me telling her she never got the concept after I told her " I told you I was going to get me revenge and you never listen" and after that Shorty still didn't understand why I did what I did and Lisha told me to stop admitting it to her so I brought up my money being stolen two weeks ago and while holding her baby Shorty kept saying she had nothing to do with it and I said the same thing to her about her money and to make another long story short Lisha talked me into giving her $60 and at the same time Lisha godmother ran me out her front door with her oldest son and we both went to Momma T house where I stayed there till Lisha friend Chick came through swooping me up right along with Lisha and took me to my house where we smoked two blunts and played cards before they left and the next day I stayed home all day. That day I got the phone call about Rae baby dying at the age of five months and since we didn't talk since 2011 I decided to hit her up seeing if she was ok. Other than that I didn't talk to no one besides Meka, Mek-mek, Mz. Trouble and the few people on my dad side of the family. Since the big fall out between Shorty and I decided not to talk to no one from that area from Tev to Man baby mana and as far as Lil Mace go I no longer trusted him and the loyalty I had for him went down the drain. Even though I didn't want to go to Rae's baby funeral thinking she too was going to set me up I decided to go and to my surprise wasn't nothing fishy jumping off nor did one see any faces from Mountview but then again it was a baby funeral so I should of trusted Rae enough that nothing was going to happen yet I was paranoid the a motherfucka. Going back home that night I linked with Lisha and back on 30th I went where I stayed a few days over Momma T house smoking with Lisha and Nita. Since Chi-chi birthday was coming in a few days I decided to get her bringing her back to 30th where she met my niece Jaja and my nephew Pooder and they all went with E-Boo over Nita house while Lisha her new friend Kash and I went to my house to start drinking and geeking and we were so geeked we entertain ourselves by playing hide-in-go-seek in the dark to playing cards since I didn't have cable installed yet. The next day I decided to take Jaja and Chi-chi back to my house instead of going to my mom b-day dinner she didn't invite me to. Even after Tez, Trey and my dad asked me was I coming I still decided against it and now I wish I didn't. Going to my house as planned I was about to get on the 79 bus but before I got on it Lisha made it known that Chi-chi wasn't on the bus already which made me scared thinking someone would kidnap her. Just then I saw the bus in front of me pulling off and GOD let me know she was on the 81 and it's like I watched my body moved dropping everything in my hand running for the bus. Even though the bus was at a red light my over dramatic ass ran to the bus attempting to open the door yet it didn't open so I ran to the front of the bus ordering the driver to open the door at the same time my shoulder got dislocated for the 3rd time yet I wasn't settle till I Chi-chi was off the bus at the next stop. I guess that was GOD way of telling me venges is His and not mines say the Lord. Meeting Lisha I had her call the EMS and waited for what seem like forever till they drove in a circle finally finding me and they escorted me back to Metro Health Hospital where I followed the same procedure getting put to sleep while they popped my shoulder back in place and finally going home 5a.m the next day exhausted. The next few days I took cautious about my shoulder and dropped Chi-chi off to her mom and went back on 30th with Lisha and we did the same shit every time we were to link up and that was to stay high. This time after leaving the hospital I made me an appointment to orthopedic follow by my therapy sessions I booked for my shoulder. This time I was told that my bone had fractured both at the top and bottom of my arm causing me to have the dislocations out of nowhere and that it was a possibility that I was to get surgery yet the doctor was focusing on my right hand saying he can also do surgery on my right hand switching my bottom bones to the top and the top bones to the bottom possibility making my hand work and that freak me out even more. Undecided on what I was going to do I took the next two weeks going to therapy sessions and started my usual therapy for my right hand and right foot so I was busy going to doctor's appointment yet since I stayed 25minute walking distance from my house to the hospital I didn't have a problem till that Tuesday after my therapy session I guess I woke up on the wrong side off the bed. Just as soon as I woke up lifting my head did my shoulder pop out of place again which pissed me off since I was supposed to clean my house that day. Laying on my stomach I began to grab my phone calling the EMS and since my house was locked up and I stayed by myself the lady on the phone stayed on the phone with me till EMS showed up getting in my house with a spare key one of my neighbors had to have yet since I wasn't dress and there were male paramedics I had to wait even longer for two females paramedic to come out. For those who don't how it hell to have a dislocation imagine someone pulling on your bone twisting it at the same time and realize it is a painful experience to go through. I mean everything on your body makes the shoulder hurt from moving your head to breathing heavy it all affected the pain in my shoulder. What's worse is it was my only good arm that was doing the pain and when your shoulder is dislocated you want be able to move your arm and if you tried the pain was extreme and even if you wanted to move your arm your shoulder would block you from moving your arm so you had no choice but to let your bone from your shoulder hang on your flesh while still attached to your lower bone so I had no choice but lay on my stomach with a tank top on and some boy shorts till the two females EMS came through, getting me dress and escorted me to the Metro again in the whole time I was in more pain then the last time. Repeating the same procedure getting happy with some medicine I was glad when it was all over yet this time they kept me over night not sending me home since I stayed by myself which wasn't safe enough. Talking to my dad that night he was supposed to come get me the next day but as the next day went by he never showed up nor did my mom answer my phone calls so I was transferred to a dirty smelly nursing home on 66th in Carnegie where I cried myself to sleep after getting settled in. The next day papa Toby visited me and talked to my mom yet no one came to discharge me. I asked papa Toby and he said no and that I needed to stay here as if I was comfortable wearing a diaper in a gown then he ate my food that I didn't want and left. Then I asked my mom crying to her and she too was no help. Then calling Lisha she too didn't come through. No one on both sides of my family came to see me, help me or let me crash at their house for a few days and I was pissed. Lucky for me on the 3rd day of my visit both Mz. Trouble and Mek-mek came to see me and after a long convocation and them witnessing how the patients were getting treated and how dirty and smelly that place was they both signed me out that Friday and we waited for Toby to pick us up and take me home that night having Mz. Trouble, Mek-mek and Chi-chi stayed there with me. That night I found out Mek-mek who we called virgin Mary was at the time was pregnant meaning she was no longer a virgin but I still ain't believe her until I saw the tears in her eyes. Waking up the next day I had my dad by some weed with my money and to drop it off at my house and as time went by I stayed in the house inviting Los over to play a card game till my dad came back with home food and my bud and some milds and as dinner was getting cooked I was waiting to get high but first I kicked Los out so I can smoke and as soon as the fried chicken, mac and cheese and broccoli was done we ate and I smoked and things seem cool till my dad pissed me off taking one of my blunts as if I wasn't paying attention. Confronting him about it he did one of them "I need this" speech and I walked away feeling embarrassed that both Mz. Trouble and Mek-mek knew what was going on and instead of him asking about the blunt he took it yet if it was the other way around he would have been pissed the fuck off. That Sunday I cleaned the house while papa Toby stopped by playing spades with us before leaving and that evening Toby came to pick Mz. Trouble and Mek-mek up bringing his friend Dope Boy with him. When Dope boy came around he liked to crack jokes and I did the same. After all was said and done he could never talk trash about my pussy not being good or fresh matter of fact none of the forty different niggas I fucked so far could tell me shit bout my pussy yet I could talk trash to a few including Dope Boy a.k.a minute men. My sugar daddy can last longer than what he did so I was ready for the joke session. As jokes were being made Toby took it upon himself to take one of my dad hotdogs putting it to his mouth but not before I snatched the hot dog from him putting it back in the pot. Then Toby grabs some newspaper and dumb it in the pot walking off making an exit and as soon as they were pulling off I dumbed the whole pot of hotdog juice on Toby truck causing it to spill on both Dope Boy and Mz. Trouble. Letting Mz. Trouble back in Dope Boy and Toby took the chance to dumb a pot of dirt in my kitchen sing not realizing it was a garbage disposal and the prank ended as Mek-mek and Mz. Trouble was cleaning the sink ass the dirt went down the garbage disposal. Over the next few days I went back on 30th just to smoke and went back home that Wednesday to meet up with a guy name Mar who been trying to fuck over a year and since I wanted some new dick I let him hit after he gave me a few blunts. The same night I had a long convocation with my #1papa not knowing that was going to be the last conversation I was going to have with him and after I hung up with him Mar and I fucked again that night then as usual I kicked his ass out going to bed that night. The next two days I went back on 30th where I sold my pain pills to one of Momma T friends and used the money to go shopping that sweetest day but not before running into a guy I call Mr. Motherfucker for a reason. As I was waiting on the bus I caught a glimpse of a tall brown skin brother dressed like he was going to an interview. At first I ain't say nothing till he came back introducing himself and I did the same and after a brief convo I gave him my number and later that night he texted me and we went through the getting to know you stage and after a few texts it was planned for him to come over that Sunday night with some liquor and weed and just as planned it was in motion as he came through with the items. Since I didn't have cable yet we made more convo as we drank on the peach 4loko and smoking on loud yet soon as my phone rang my attention went from him to Mz. Trouble who was on the phone yet as soon as I asked why was Mr. Motherfucker staring at me his response got me off the phone real quick. After him telling me he felt like eating my pussy I lead him into the room where under five minutes did this nigga make me cum and is voted as my 2nd best head doctor. After I came I gave him my back shots and he talked me into letting him spend the night. As he was holding me I couldn't get no sleep and as soon as 7clock hit, I woke his as up and kicked him out. The plan was to treat him like I did Mar yet after getting dress he asked me not to let this be a one night stand and he really enjoyed my company so he say so, I let him hit the next weekend unlike Mar I never planned on fucking him again and far as Los he wasn't hitting no time soon. I even let D'Nell finally come over after a lot of begging I let him come and I fucked him and as usual he ate the box and the nigga never came empty handed and he too also spend a night in my bed for the 1st and only time. Just a few days later did he get shot four times and had to go to Metro yet he was mad at me for not visiting him during his stay. Instead I got my box braids done by Lisha and went back home bringing Jaja and Pooder with me meeting Tez his old gf Lex and Cash at my house. Since Cash ain't smoke it was just the three of us smoking Michigan weed till Cash left. After that we all went to bed and the next day Lex went back to her hometown leaving Tez here to celebrate his birthday. That Halloween we got the effect of a hurricane across a shore called Arlene and the effect was bad that we got hit thousand miles away. I saw from lights going out to tress being broke to part of my mom roof was missing. In the meantime Tez and I stayed high meeting fake bud men on my street to even using Mr. Motherfucka for his liquor and weed and the next day Danny (tink sister) came through giving us the news that she was pregnant this time keeping the baby. After the hurricane was over Tez went to our mom house where he chilled at for the remainder of the day and after another night of Mr. Motherfucker spending the night I went over my mom house that Nov6, 2012 and voted for the first time and afterwards I bought some food for Tez to cook and afterwards I went back home. The next two days I stayed at home but that Friday I grabbed Chi-chi, Pooder and Jaja and took them all to my house where they spent the weekend at my house either playing in my hair to watching t.v and that Sunday they all left having my house empty yet not even 30 minutes past till D'Nell popped up at my house still wearing his bandages from the gun womb. Letting him come in I let it be known for his disrespect towards me and my dad side of the family that we wasn't fucking no more nor were we ever going to be on good terms all because he let his anger get to him when I didn't visit him in the hospital and after I fucked him for the last time I meant that shit. Same time Mr. Motherfucker called to let me know he was on his way to my house so I had to kick D'Nell out and hopped in the shower before Mr. Motherfucker came through with the usual 4locko and bud and I let him fuck that night as well and he did the same spending the night procedure and I did the same kicking him out that next morning just so I can get some sleep and his visit were more frequent. As Thanksgiving rolled around I left with papa Toby and my dad to see my aunty and her family where we watched as my uncle deep fried the turkey and we watched outside as we were drinking on my aunty margarita mixed smoking on some loud and I enjoyed myself and coming to Cleveland we all went over my other aunt house with my uncle Dirt and there four kids plus Dirt brother Fuddy where we watched a football game before going home calling it a night. As the next few weeks came about I chilled with Mr. Motherfucker for the most part. I even went over my dad new girlfriend house who stayed down the street from me and would go over there smoking and drinking till Mr.Motherfucker was close by and we did the usual me using him to get under the influence never letting him hit my blunts and he did the head game on point and I gave him those back shots and after he stayed the night only this time I was getting more comfortable with the guy. I even started to sleep through the night, not the whole night but at least a bitch got some sleep but every morning I still kicked his ass out so I can do what I do which was go over Mz. Trouble mom house who she moved back with or my dad new girlfriend house people call her Midnight meeting two of her kids. I even decided to spend Christmas with Mr. Motherfucker yet the day before Christmas this fool went to jail for stealing and explained the reason for him not showing up. Since my granny died I never cared for the holidays, I just wanted to not be alone lucky for me the same cousin who invited me to the family reunion back in August was the same one who invited me over for a plate and I did just that chilling with some cousins of mine till I went home that night. As the year was ending I went to get my hair done for the new year new me look aptitude and since I was doing ok since the shit that happened in May I was on a whole new aptitude and after going over Momma T new house since 30th was about to get torn down I took down my braids the next two days and got a relaxer the 3rd day showing off my real hair and I left planning on using Los for his weed since Mr. Motherfucker was in jail still yet little did I know he was out the same night I called Los to come over. Almost going home Mr. Motherfucker called me letting me know he was on his way and since Los ain't have a cell phone at the time I couldn't tell him never mind nor did I want nether boys to know they wasn't the only ones. Just as Mr. Motherfucker came through I ran into Los as I was getting some bud with Mr. Motherfucker money and I had to tell Los never mind about coming over not explaining my reason and neither did he ask he just went about his way while I entertain Mr. Motherfucker till he left that December 31st. That night I brought the New Year with uncle Dirt and his family and I had a blast and was even more excited that

I would be turning 21 this year. Starting 2013 off it seemed cool not knowing how this year was going to turn out. For starts I was schedule a Botox injection the day after my b-day and till then I was going to kick it to hide the nervousness I had built up inside me. First Midnight and I got our tongue pierced and since I threw my tongue ring out after fighting Mz. Trouble for the last time this would be my 2nd time and it didn't even hurt the second time around like it did before. That night I even gave Mr. Motherfucker a blow job for the first time showing off my tongue ring. I even linked back up with my Sugar daddy this time he got off of work at 530a.m getting to my house at 540a.m each time giving me the same weed and money and in return I let him do his three minute stroke game and we were both satisfied and I smoked the weed either with my dad, or Mr. Motherfucker if not by myself. I even met a new bud guy through my dad who took an interest in me yet I took interest in the free weed he was giving me yet I didn't fuck him yet instead I used his company to get me high. I literally spent my days towards my b-day having different boys come in and out one day was an unexpected day yet I got through it. Inviting Los over again for the 4th time I used him to get high till Mr. Motherfucker let me know he was on his way instead as time went by Mr. Motherfucker called me letting me know he was at the door which pissed me off. Since it was one way in and way out I was trying to come up with a plan to not have them two see each other than the chance came and I decided to put Los and the cubby hole explaining to him that my ex-boyfriend just got out of jail and needed a place to crash at. Lying to him he did what I said and as I let Mr. Motherfucker in he asked what took me so long so I ignored him leading him upstairs. Scared out my mind getting caught up I started kissing on Mr. Motherfucker leading him to my bedroom as I directed Los to let himself out locking my bottom lock is as the plan came about and it all went into motion and I fucked Mr. Motherfucker that night letting him hold me something I got use to and realized that the love I wanted to from Tev that I use to get from him I slowly was getting from Mr. Motherfucker and that began pissing me off. I also noticed Mr. Motherfucker weekends visit became to make his visits throughout the week having me work around his schedule. Besides chilling with my bud man Black who gave me a puppy and sugar daddy I got back in contact with "Kid" who let me in on the break up between him and his girlfriend yet I didn't believe him at the time nor did I care since I wanted to fuck him just as bad as he wanted to fuck me little did he know I had change of feelings for him and instead of the girl who craved his attention to the girl who went with the flow of her own. I got to know Black and from how he was talking I realized he talked about himself a little too much which was a turn off for me so I had him in his own personal category. As my b-day rolled around I had Mz. Trouble take me out to eat and had her buy me a bottle and I chilled over Midnight house with my dad buy as the day of my b-day came around I only went to stay high with my dad since I couldn't get a drink nor eat after a certain time since I was getting put to sleep as the Botox was injected in me the same time my dad was embarrassing me by playing "Booty Me Down" to "Turn Up by 2Chainz and the doctor thought it was funny then to piss me off he told Mr. Motherfucker I was going for surgery which I wasn't planning on telling anyone till it actually happened and afterwards I went to do my financial aid having my dad sign it since I was planning on going to school that August. That evening after buying some liquor and bud did my dad get arrested for tail gating causing me to walk home from Fullerton the same night I found out Tez and Lex was in jail on my birthday thanks to a drug bust in West Vagina where he was at. After I walked with Midnight home I drunk some liquor and smoke two blunts with her before leaving going home to meet Mr. Motherfucker at my house just to fuck him. We spent the remainder of that month using each other for our own personal reason slowly getting hipped to Mr. Motherfucker and his situation he didn't tell me yet. For starters I found out he lost his job when he went to jail and never told me yet it was obvious then to make him sound more sad he told me that he goes to the blood bank to donate blood 2x a week getting 200$ a month which he been doing since he was 18 and since he was now 26 at the time he been doing our for a while and explained the mark he had in the middle of his arm. Thirdly I got hipped to him stealing movies out of either Walgreen or Rite aid selling them to either Buy backs or Fye getting five dollars for each movie cashing in three at a time. The fucked up part bout it he thought I wasn't going to find out as if I wasn't going to ask questions. Even though I knew that I still felt bad for him and his past from being a crack baby though being adopted to him having his first heartbreak something I never experience relationship wise I looked down on him as if he was less of a person and felt sorry for him but I didn't let that shit show. The nigga even poured his heart out yet that didn't stop me from doing me. Last time I checked a bitch was still single and got the hang of the mingle game. I still fucked other people from "Kid" to my sugar daddy who came early as hell but I had a happy as day smoking his different weed and spending his money on weed. I ended up writing Mr. Motherfucker a letter telling him if he felt the way he said he felt then he had to prove to me he the men I want/need him to be. All he had to do was find another job and prove to me that he's stable by June and since it was the middle of Feb he had four months which is way enough time to get the ball running. I decided to give him the letter on Valentine day yet he never called nor showed up so I made it a mental note to give him the next time I see him and I celebrated Valentine day off with my sugar daddy coming through that morning with a pot of roses, some weed and a card and after I opened it was 50$ in it. After chilling with him for a minute I decided to stop by Midnight house to smoke with her and my dad before going back home on the way I ran into my bud men Dre who gave me a flower and a card . Going home I ran into Black who was with the puppy he had staying with me and after smoking and chilling with him I finally bust it open giving him back shots and that nigga had a style of his own and felt good as fuck. Just as expected Mr. Motherfucker came the next day and after letting him read the letter he claim he would change yet only time will tell and in the meantime I was still doing me starting off with an old friends from high school and truth be told I had better then what he gave me. Donny (his name) wasn't whack but he could do better yet what pissed me off was he left a hickey on my neck yet I dig the aggressive shit. I had to wear Mr. Motherfucker t-shirt to cover the mark up when Mr. Motherfucker came. He was slow enough not to notice it nor did I have sex with him for a few days. I felt like because of his situation he was using me for sex and I used him for his head, the food he brought, and he supplied the weed and I never smoked with him at that time minus a few events and as long as he let me treat him like that I allowed it and on the days he wasn't hear I was doing my own unpredictable as day. I also kept him around to avoid the loneness feeling I been feeling a year almost. Midnight daughter Jessica started to hang with me and I introduced her to several friends from Man who she fucked 2x to lil Mace attempting to fuck him to "kid" who we did a threesome with to my sugar daddy and of course there was Mr. Motherfucker. Things were cool yet the day after Mr. Motherfucker b-day things shocked the fuck out of me. The night of his b-day I chilled with him and his older brother who I met before and Jessica came along and long story short after getting interrupted earlier by his brother as I was receiving head, I was cool when went in my room after his brother fell asleep and proceed back to orgasms he me. Waking up the next day I got the shocking news about Mr. Motherfucker fucked his biological mother thanks to Mr. Motherfucker brother telling Jessica and her telling me. After getting told what Mr. Motherfucker brother he repeated what Jessica told me and I felt disgusted. I waited till the next time I seen him to discuss the topic but now I wish I didn't know. After describing the story what I couldn't get was him saying her ass was bigger than mines yet what put the icing on the cake was he fucking her from the back to both them performing oral sex on each other. The story went like this.... When he was eighteen, he finally met his mom and other kids(him the youngest)and an in Georgia drinking and smoking at the hotel they were staying in and suppose he stayed home while all his siblings went out. Then he decided to do what he was told and put grease in her hair which turned him on then to the massage of her back he was doing then the fucking began not till she sucked his dick and he ate his mom box and long story short they bust their nuts after hitting it from the back. Then had the nerve to say his mom seduced it. I guess he had to go back in what he came out of. What pissed me off is I been fucking and sucking this nigga dick it couldn't get any worse than that but it did thanks his brother stealing some money written for the landlord his second visit and thought I wasn't going to find out yet GOD had my back and the same day he took it was the same day he lost it and I too didn't pay rent the of the month March .What shocked me is Mr. Motherfucker informed me of the act and I couldn't get mad since he already warned me to put up my stuff up yet I forgot I left the money order in the box cards that was left on my table. Just so happen I became sick after I got caught in the rain and spending night at Midnight house going home the next night. Not even a week past and I was back in the hospital vomiting anything that came down my throat. Thinking I was going home that night they kept me for observations as I was on meds and still vomiting. Since I left Mr. Motherfucker in my house thinking I was coming back I had my dad kick him out my house as my dad locked my house up for me as I told my dad to come up to the hospital and the next thing I know was Mr. Motherfucker waking me up. Instead of my dad being here to discharge me Mr. Motherfucker set with me as he too witness the vomiting when the nurse injected me with the medicine and not even five seconds after the injection did I vomit again. Since he couldn't stay long I had him walk to Midnight house to get the key from my dad while I waited to get discharged 8a.m that morning and was put on a clear liquid diet where Mr. Motherfucker catered to my every need from buying the applesauce and Jell-O from the store to keeping me high and I gave him his respect for that. See I know you'll wonder why I was still with him. Tell you the truth I had my reasons from using him for his sex,, weed, and the little money he had to feeling the way Tev use to make me feel so I replaced Tev with Mr. Motherfucker accepting his flaws and all and I honestly felt bad for the guy and sometimes looked down on him because I knew he could do better. The nigga was smart and always came with plans and ideas yet he was lazy and like to have fun doing what me or his brother said and his life was based on others. In returned I knew he used me for my sex and a place to crash and he went from coming over from being here 3/4 nights out the week to every night through the month of March slowly moving in and as looking as he gave me what I want and I still did what I did I was cool with it all. This here was my life instead of being round family or having a job. I even put him through my personal test I put every nigga I fucked recently through just because I don't trust people and although he passed some the ones he failed told me he was a person who procrastinate and think about himself often and it tools me where his head was at in life yet he was irresponsible. Still stuck on the fact he fucked his mom I told both Mz. Trouble and Meka yet Mz. Trouble ran her mouth telling everyone I knew including Mek-mek, Sin, Juju, Toby, Man who told "kid" before I told him and that told me not to tell her certain shit. Things were going cool and even had a babysitting job watching my two cousins and sometimes watching two more kids in Maple. I figured I could use the extra money to treat myself yet that wasn't the only money I received. Since I considered Mr. Motherfucker as a boyfriend after March I still cheated but I had to get more out of it then a nut so the best thing next to sex is money. I went from fucking my neighbor who stayed behind me name JB to a guy who I met through Jessica who she also fucked the difference is I got money and weed out of it while she did it for free. I would literally kick Mr. Motherfucker out my house that morning doing whatever he did that day and invite a nigga over on the days I wanted to cheat then go out to Maple to babysit then go home and be entertain my t.v. or Mr. Motherfucker and on weekends I was free to do as I pleased. Things were better than before and I thought it would get better yet I was hit with an unexpected call from Lex saying my mom was in the hospital as I was in the tub on a Saturday morning. Getting straight out the tub I called papa Toby to give me a ride to South Pointe hospital since he was around the corner yet he didn't want to instead Midnight gave me a ride to the bus stop close to downtown and I met up with Mz. Trouble telling her the news and payed a friend name Liv to take me the rest of the way and as soon as I went to her room the sight of her being sedated with a machine controlling her breathing had tears and my eyes as I cried. I was mad at her for not telling me my great aunt died back in January missing her funeral and now I was scared to death that she was next since I knew she been sick for a while now. What pissed me of was that I had to explain who I was to the nurses since my mom only told them she had two kids knowing she had four yet I was still sad of the condition she was in being sedated with a breathing tube down her throat. The sight of her breathing with the machine help put tears in my eyes and after leaving that night I went out to the 49th bar with Mek-mek, ,Liv, Mz. Trouble, and Man drinking absolute and smoking on gas since I just got paid and had money to blow. That was the only way besides sex that relive stress and the times I escape reality. The second day we went our again only this time as we were at 55th marathon gas station were there shots fired and I was in a panic after arguing with Mek-mek on who was sitting in the middle yet as soon as the sound of gunshots coming from who knows where were hopped in the car as Liv drove or the back way taking me home. All I could think about GOD watching over me and my mom possibly dying. Luckily for her she was awoken with an oxygen mask on so she couldn't talk and guess was the first person she seen.....me. Since she couldn't talk we used pen and paper. The shit she let me know telling me my siblings were over cousins of ours house and doing the run around on the free time I had I found out Tink was with (what people say) the hoe the family house and instead of going to school which she went to Kenney she was babysitting three kids at the park and Boggie was over the hoe of the family grandmother house and since he was still being home school instead of being at home to do his work he was forced to leave the house leaving Starr and new dog name Nyla in the house alone. What pissed me off is my own family as they say we're making it impossible for me to get both my siblings and they were behind on their school work thanks to my mom telling Boogie to tell people about a no contact order that expired back in 2011.Then was also a rumor that I called the hoe of the family grandmother a bitch which was a lie her grandkids made. Honestly to keep it 100 I don't give a fuck about no one grandmother being alive technically simply because my granny was dead and I will forever miss her so to think I was going to have a convo about another person grandmother wasn't happening. Pissed the fuck off I let Tez handle the situation after he quit his job and back to Cleveland he went and him and our godmother solved the situation by getting both my siblings and bringing them back at home. I went from selling pussy to being bother by Mr. Motherfucker. Finally my mom went home and after a few days she back to the hospital this time going to Metro this time my #1papa was in the hospital slowly dying yet I didn't see it. Doing the same shit as before I went for liquor and weed having my own version of a party. One time we went downtown to hit the bars going bar hopping till we decided to go back to my house but not before running into Mr. Motherfucker talking to some girl as I watched him wrap his arm around the girl's waste. Instead of causing seen I waited for the bus and soon I got on the bus I watched as he got on the bus not realizing I was on the bus till he seen me leaving the girl on the bus with her male friend and noticed we all got off at same stop. I'm not going to lie I was pissed at the fact that he made me look bad but not as bad I was going to make him look. See I knew I was doing me but by him slowly moving in my house staying under my roof he should of never did what he did and felt he had no respect being he needed me and I wasn't having that. That night and the next day I ignored his text and phone calls yet I did send him a text telling him I ain't mad more disappointed that I expect more from here. That following Sunday I finally decided to meet with him to talk to him having him tell me everything from fucking his older brother other baby mother that Easter the same time I cheated on him for money. Then he explained his reason for being downtown all because he assumed I was ignoring his calls while I was stuck over papa Toby house after I was supposed to visit my mom and since my phone was dead and I had no charger the plans I set for us to go to the movies were canceled and instead of Mr. Motherfucker coming to my house he went downtown to the bar and casino meeting an old friend till he seen me on the bus. The creepy part was that he got on another bus just to beat me to my house hiding in some bushes by the bus stop watching me as I walked home with Tez and Scooter going back to the girl house the night he ain't come to my house. After telling me that and catching him in his lies I no longer felt bad on cheating on him and it wasn't going to stop no time soon. At the end of the day my main focus was on my mom and her getting out the hospital. I finally let Mr. Motherfucker come back in but I was using him as always and the game between who can play the sex game better began. I decided to fuck Black who I been fucking from time to time the but this time we fucked at the graveyard by my house on West44th bending over a tombstone having my juice flow on his 9inch dick and nigga felt good as he stoked the inside of my tunnel just to fuck. I also gave him his puppy back for my own reason. I also fucked him only because Mr. Motherfucker was pissing me off thirsty for me to get some weed from him, Tez and I to smoke so today was Black lucky day and afterwards I went home and hopped in the shower while Tez rolled up the weed Mr. Motherfucker bought. I also had my one friend Donny from South high school who left the hickey on my neck letting him meet Jessica yet she had plans of her own inviting "kid" and his brother Lil Mace over having me feel embarrassed telling Donny I'll catch him later and him telling me that I owe him yet I didn't care since I was now about to entertain "kid" things entertain I hit some. Jessica even began watching me have sex with Mr. Motherfucker and I let her one time getting a phone call from my Sweetheart and thanks to Jessica answering the phone he heard my moans which made me stop having sex just to give him my undivided attention and after I said a few words I went back to fucking Mr. Motherfucker knowing my Sweetheart heard me. Things were cool yet when the last week of May hit it was a rude awakening for me and my three out of four side of the family. It started off with my older cousin who I share the same birthday with got shot for no reason that Saturday then that following Tuesday papa Toby dad died then that Thursday was the day my #1papa died and that hit my heart the same way it did when his wife died. What pissed me off is that I got the news from Tez who left to go to Michigan after my mom was released from the hospital a week before my #1papa died. That day I wanted to destroy my house but instead I left the house to meet up with my dad after falling out with him since this was his second time calling me a handicap bitch. Meeting him in the same graveyard I fucked Black in we walked to Midnight house where I cried in my dad's arm as Black and someone else were around to comfort me and after I cried for a while we got high and Black gave me extra weed to smoke. I was planning on staying yet my dad and Midnight were arguing so I left going back home where I met Mr. Motherfucker who pissed me off thinking I was lying about the three males who died in a week. Going to all three funerals the last week of May my#1 papa was first and guess who decided to show up Mrs. Hoe of the family. Walking in with Missty and her husband who I thought was just a friend at first until I found out the baby she had was his. I sat by my mom since she was crying and I peeped both Cash and Moochie didn't speak while Spanky spoke and I rode with him to our family gravesite where we watched him get buried and we decided to see my granny using some off my#1papa flowers putting it over her tombstone and just as predicted Spanky, my mom, Tink and I cried as we left going to one of#1papa other daughter house where I saw Mrs. hoe of the family and slowly but surely I was going to fuck with her since I was hurt, mad and wanted to fight someone so I choose her since she was talking shit bout my mom when she was in the hospital. At first I spoke to a few people and started drinking Absolute letting everyone I was now 21 and I had uncle Spanky roll up some weed and relaxed till I rode with uncle Spanky wife to drop my mom off and as soon as I was back I started fucking with Mrs. hoe of the family by talking shit and as soon as she walked past me to get in the house I hit her with a kid hockey stick I don't remember how I got it but anyways I hit her 2x starting a fight yet Moochie was right behind Mrs. Hoe pushing her in the house as I was getting pushed back separating me from Mrs. Hoe of the family and long story short after more words were being said and letting everyone I wanted to fight till the daughter who house the party was at threatened uncle Spanky saying she will grab her gun to shoot him if we don't leave and as soon as Spanky said "well you going to have to shoot me" I stood right next to him and we caught her bluff for she never came with a gun but we did leave just in case maple police was coming. The next day I went on my dad side of the family to a dinner and met cousins from out of town drinking and geeking that night and that nice as house we were at and I went home preparing for the other funerals that Saturday. Waking up Saturday I got high and had my dad take me to my family home church on my mom side and talk to a few family members before leaving knowing I couldn't stay the whole visit and after leaving I went to Midnight house where I waited on some cousins and my dad to get dress for my great grandad funeral that afternoon getting high on the way and after I popped a pill got drunk over my papa Toby house and went home with one of my cousins yet we walked in to Mr. Motherfucker surprising me but as naked in my dining room and by him not knowing I was bringing my cousin with me that was also gay which pissed me off. That night though I got high with my cousin, getting him geeked since I couldn't go to sleep. As the next few days went by, I got hip to my uncle Curtis wife not needing me too babysit the kids no more since she didn't come up front and tell me yet I didn't care since it was warm out I was chilling. Just because I was grieving over my#1papa yet I still did me and making Mr. Motherfucker look bad and since I had free time since my days were unpredictable yet cool. Still seeing my sugar daddy his work schedule changes getting off at 4:30pm I would see him on his lunch break since he works downtown at 12p.m I would make myself available for him 3to4 times a week and when I went with him I chilled with different guys fucking for money and weed or both .I went from meeting a dude at the library and even though he was good I never fucked him again since he bust his nut inside me knowing the condom broke and not telling me till after he bust his nut. I did meet a few Westside niggas even chilling with this cool white dude even meeting his family yet I never fucked him I just used him for his loud smoking with him and his uncle who had kidney failure like my mom. Other days I went over Mz. Trouble house on kinsman. Being over there was just as unpredictable as mines and at first things was cool having her, Shay to Mek-mek and since she and Toby just broke up she had male friends over and we would smoke, drink and talk shit and each night will go home every night chilling with Mr. Motherfucker. Things were going cool till the day Cece pissed me off again. On this day in June things were the same as I brought weed and since the guys that was there had drinks and we were all on the porch with their kids while Mrs. Trouble was explaining her breakup story between Toby and her saying after she and him was arguing over who was putting what CD on the Xbox and Toby wanted to play the game while Mz. Trouble wanted to exercise. Toby then decided to leave and play the game over Dope boy house to end the argument but to add fuel though the fire Mz. Trouble wanted him to take Lil Tony who she had back in March yet when Toby was leaving, Mz. Trouble was yelling telling Toby to take the 3 month old baby leaving the infant on the porch saying "take the motherfucka" walking back in the house leaving Toby take baby saying she's unfit and that did the breakup. Anyway as we're chilling Cece jumped in the convo I was having between me and Shay. Then turned around and brought the topic about being stranded in Michigan saying "if it wasn't for her I would be there being stranded still" as if she was the only way out and what pissed me off is that I paid Cece her money back so why the fuck was she bringing up something that happen thirteen months ago. Then I had to let her now she was the first convenient option and not to take that role to the head. This is one example of when I say both sisters Mz. Trouble and Cece will act tough in front of people to as if I am a soft bitch and is one of the three reasons I fight for I mentioned in my 1st book . I was still grieving already that my#1papa died last month and to make matters worse Cece kept talking this time getting in my face. At first I was told I hit Cece first and that stared the fight. As I was sitting on the steps I defended myself as Cece thought again for the second time only this time she managed to get on top of me punching me dead in the eye yet I squirmed from underneath her and proceeded to drag her ass down the stairs since she had a hold on my box braids. Grabbing both her legs with my one arm we were in a locked position as she was two stairs away from the ground as she was pulling on my hair causing five braids to come out yet I never let go till the group of guys who was watching separated the two of us as I notice everyone on that street was outside. After calming down Shay and I bought some peach Amsterdam and after drinking I went home and notice Mr. Motherfucker not there nor did I call him to see where he was at. The next two days I avoided his calls and linked up with Lisha for her to redo some of my braids to cover the three bald spots I had in my hair. Finally letting him come back knowing he really ain't have nowhere to go I let him know if he piss me off again then I'm kicking him out but I guess that went over his head since he pissed met off two days later as I was on my way dropping Pooder off. Since Mr. Motherfucker had to go to his program I went to Fye to trade in movies and was only giving him 5$ keeping 10$ on me yet we got into an argument about me giving him his money yet I ignored him as I got on the healthline having him followed me to Lisha house not going to his program and as soon as I got off of the bus I handed him all his money and told him his stuff would be outside by the time he get back and walked off yet he followed me to Lisha house where he gave me the punk as 10$ and me and Lisha smoked a blunt in her room while

Mr. Motherfucker was in the living room with my sister E-boo till we all left going over Momma T house but not before Mr. Motherfucker damn near followed me not leaving till I gave him his kids and told him I love him. Truth be told I liked the attention. Few days later Spanky came to visit for his own personal reason and him,, Scooter, and I linked up and kicked it. That was also around the same time uncle Curtis money was stolen somehow which means I couldn't get the money they still old me for babysitting. I'm not no detective but let me find out someone stole my uncle Curtis bank card withdrawing money meaning someone knew his password to his cards. How about the fact that his card was stolen from his house where only him his wife and two kids stayed at. It's cool cause everyone including me on my dad side of the family who knows my uncle wife knows his wife was the reason behind this just like she was the reason for papa Toby bank cards being stolen by getting uncle Curtis drunk and his wife and her1st baby father used the cards a few years back to she's might be the reason to uncle Curtis getting jumped. Everyone seen it but Uncle Curtis which pissed of a lot of people. Back to the story Spanky and I chilled at my house since my mom was the reason Spanky for a ticket for parking in my mom handicap parking spot by her house for who knows what so we stayed high till I ran out on that Tuesday yet Black came through giving me free weed and after having Mr. Motherfucker but some shells Spanky and I smoked in front of Mr. Motherfucker face. Ever since that incident in May and him not coming over last week I started to treat Mr. Motherfucker as he deserved in my eyes from spitting in his noodles a couple times that he ate every day since I never let him eat my food and the food he brought over I cooked occasionally for the both of us. I still will smoke my weed with me and smoke up all his weed and the cheating never stopped. Shit again since he allowed to be treated as such I did as he pleased. That Wednesday since I didn't have money or weed I decided to get it from my sugar daddy since Wednesdays is his payday and as planned I met him downtown while Spanky was at the library and when I got the money and gave him a quick blow job and I use the money to buy a quarter and Spanky a pack of Newport and we smoked till that Friday when Spanky left going back home and I felt sad all over again but Tez was coming up here for the holiday so I was looking forward to that and getting high and drunk with my brother. Till then I had my fun yet thanks to Mr. Motherfucker my plans were changed again when he wasn't supposed to come over the day I had Los cone over. Since Los had his1st baby he had to drop some diapers off leaving his nightcap over yet when he was on his way back so was Mr. Motherfucker both getting on the 79 which pissed me of figuring I had to come up with a plan fast nor wanting them walking the same way to my house. Thank goodness it didn't take long before I came up with a plan calling Mr. Motherfucker telling him to meet me two stops before my stop meeting me at the park. Same time since Los didn't have a phone I wrote him a letter saying I had though go somewhere leaving his clothes outside. Meeting Mr. Motherfucker at the park I slowly walked home nervous if I was going to see Los but when I got to the house his clothes nor him was and sight and that night I fucked Mr. Motherfucker only this time he tried something new from eating my ass to putting an ice cube in my pussy follow by his dick and boy did that feel good.

Chapter 6

A few days later Tez and his girlfriend came in town as planed and as soon as they went to my house the smoking process began. While we waited on Scooter, Lex and I went to get drinks and meeting Mr.Motherfucker on the way and when I got home Scooter was there and the kick back session began. As the five of us took shots and smoke weed till after 12 clock where we went to the Horseshoe casino where I won my first 10$ and my scary ass quit cashing out my money ready to go. Afterwards we went to the steelyard to I-hop to Walmart to burn time and I didn't go home to six that morning going to bed just to wake up and drink and smoke again planning to go out that night yet all I remember that night is waking up the next day salty ass fuck I ain't go out and even more mad that Tez was leaving .We spent that day giving Lex a tour of the flats getting high and after eating Chinese food and going to a bar for drinks till it was time for Tez to leave and I went home waiting on Mr. Motherfucker to come from the blood bank. As the rest of July took effect things were cool. I kept myself busy during the day going either over Lisha house to Mz. Trouble house sometimes and went home at night to Mr. Motherfucker and, the days I stayed at home I chilled with my different few male friends for my own personal reason and things were going find. I even stopped by my mom house for Tink birthday but I didn't stay long. Things were find up till the day I dislocated my shoulder for the 5th time now. Literally as soon as I got in the pool on this hot sunny day doing two strokes I felt my bone slowly go out of socket as I was under water. Not trying to cause a scene I told Jessica to inform the lifeguards of the situation and the same time keeping it cool since the guy I was flirting with only because I could see he had a big package through his boxers. As the EMS were being called another lifeguard had everyone get out the pool besides me as we waited for the EMS to arrive. At first EMS was giving me a hard time not wanting to get their suits wet yet these people was unaware that I only had one hand to use so I had to explain myself. Thankful a cute lifeguard came to grab me out the pool sitting me on the chair till I was put on a stretcher. Thinking I was going through the same procedure I was unaware of the sudden bump in the path way that caused my shoulder to pop back in place since I was strap down my shoulder had no choice but to pop it back in place causing me to scream loud in the hallway area as the pain hit yet after a few seconds the pain of my dislocation of the shoulder was gone thank GOD. Still getting sent to the emergency room I got another cat scan but not before flipping out in the bathroom punching the walls and mirror because of the wait time limit. After I got seen I was released. Waiting on my ride to go home I met two entertaining guys still wearing my hospital gown in a cast yet they wasn't my type. As the next few weeks went by I took everything easy retaining my shoulder and was told my surgery date the first week of August if I wanted to prevent future dislocations so I had no choice but to do it taking the date august 21,2013 and till then I was going to preoccupied myself up till that date. Undecided on what I was going to do Mr. Motherfucker said he would help me yet I didn't trust him as much as he thought so I made other arrangements by calling Tez asking him to come down here the day before my surgery and at first he didn't want to but as the days went by he changed his mind not knowing the real reason at that time. While mentally preparing for my surgery in two weeks I decided to have fun while it lasted not knowing how surgery was going to turn out. For starters I went with Mr. Motherfucker to the county fair in Bureau with my mom and two siblings and even though Mr. Motherfucker was pissing me off acting like a big kid I had fun having him pay for everything to him winning a contest to me staying high and after going home to eat pizza I left and went home. I went and spent time with my sugar daddy to chilling with other guys using them for their weed to even hooking back up with Tev only this time this visit was different. After talking to Tev for a while one time while on the phone with Tev Mr.Motherfucker started giving me head just like he did when I was on the phone with my mom and just like her I hung up on Tev not wanting him to hear me moan. Little did Mr. Motherfucker know I was inviting Tev over and I did just that. Just as Tev planned we fucked after him giving me head yet this time the feeling I use to feel from Tev was different. I really didn't know what it was but something was off. Since I was supposed to spend that day taking my hair down I was behind knowing my hair was supposed to be taken down already to make it look like I was doing my hair all day I went over Jessica house where she help me take my hair down just in time for me to meet Mr. Motherfucker at my door. Thinking things were going good it was the opposite. While my hair had conditioning I found out Tev left a corner piece of the condom on my floor and I picked it up putting it in my bra. Since Mr. Motherfucker was slow when it came to me creeping I thought I was going to get away with it even after it fell out my bra and on the floor in-front of him I quickly step on it sliding it to the trash without him noticing my action yet as I was watching my hair off was I informed that I cheated on him with him holding the condom wrapper that I purposely put by the trash which was telling me that Jessica snitch on me to Mr. Motherfucker telling him I fucked Tev. Not knowing what I was going to do I did the only thing I could do that my mom taught me and that was to fake cry and that's what I did apologizing and since he already knew how I felt bout Tev I made excuses. Even though I was crying I wasn't crying about me cheating on him but my life just like how I fake cried to Midnight talking her to let Jessica spend the night so she can fuck. I cried in Mr. Motherfucker arms till he kissed me and long story short we had one of many bomb sex that night. The next day I kicked Jessica out and our lil friendship she thought she had with me was now gone and on the strength I ain't want to hear my dad voice I didn't fight Jessica yet I wanted to for her telling Mr.Motherfucker. That day I went to get my hair done by Lisha telling her the story about me cheating on Mr.Motherfucker then met Mr.Motherfucker downtown going home that night. Waking up that Monday I met my mom and siblings at the zoo where Mr.Motherfucker embarrassed me by telling my mom to bystanders that I cheated on with Tev yet what made it feel worse was my mom cracking jokes about how Tev looked like comparing him to an elephant. What made me more upset is when we went to my pre surgery appointment that afternoon. Unfortunately for me the embarrassments didn't stop at the zoo but carried on through the visit telling other patients that I cheated on him to telling the nurses making me look like the bad person in the relationship. Pissed off I was supposed to go straight downtown yet I went home where Mr. Motherfucker followed me and that's' where the argument started. I went from him having his foster mom talk to me to him asking me did I cheat on him to breakup with him before my surgery. Since that was a stupid question I ignored him. After the convo I had with Scooter I decided to meet up with Scooter to go to the show called "Now you see me". Since I had a week left till surgery I went back and forth from Lisha house to Mz Trouble informing us about the beef between her and the red hair neighbor and from what I heard Mz. Trouble wasn't on fighting the red hair girl how she was to Juju or me. I even went to Mz. Trouble people house on 55th and had a blast. Since my surgery was less than five days I decided to check in on school and do my classes yet I found out I couldn't take the curses unless I pay my loan off so I was fucked. The day before my surgery day Tez came through bringing Lez with him and all their clothes as we all got prepare for my surgery date. See I thought the surgery will take a three month recovery so I expected for them to stay that long as well. The first night of them being here we walked around my Westside neighborhood getting high that night before going back in the house. On a last minute I had to reschedule my surgery from that Tuesday the 21st of August to that Wednesday August 22nd. The day before the surgery I also got my usual depo shot to avoid periods. Talking Lex with me downtown I ran into Mek-mek getting off the bus from work and her plan was to go to Mz. Trouble house and I sort of wanted to go but decided against it. Same time I seen my youngest sister on my dad side selling candy with her two older brothers along with Mr. Motherfucker yet since me and my little sister mom fell out last year over a misunderstanding that she think I stole her Obama minute phone giving it to my dad which was a lie yet she thought I did and because of that I could no longer see my little sister. After seeing my little sister her mom rudely came over to grab her and instead of causing a scene I walked off headed home where I met my dad and my brother at my house and that night all four of us got high and I went to bed prepared to wake up 6am the next morning. Waking up the next day wasn't as smoothly as I planned or wanted it to be. For starters the van was over an hour late then literally after Mr. Motherfucker and I got in the van the driver had an altercation with me telling me I had to get off his van and wait till another company van picked me up while the driver had to pick up handicap people as if I wasn't disabled myself. Since my appointment was 15minutes away I decided against his request having both Mr. Motherfucker and I stay in the van. Then the driver had the nerve to tell his boss about the switch yet when I called his company no one knew what he was talking about and neither did the driver hand me his phone demanding to speak to the person he was speaking to instead he called the police on me yet that didn't make me move. After the police got here the driver send them both away finally taking me to my doctor appointment making me 45minutes late. The only thing I was waiting on was the good old drugs getting put to sleep and the only thing I remember next was hearing my last name saying a room was ready for me for some reason I thought I was going to jail or something and I woke up fully realizing I was still at General Hospital getting escorted to a room where I spend the night there along with Mr. Motherfucker and the pain I felt after the surgery was severe yet I stayed high off of morphine and after five seconds of it kicking in I felt the drugs. My short stay I made sure I was on pain killers just so I wouldn't feel the pain and go to sleep. The doctors wanted to keep me another day but since I had Mr.Motherfucker with me I decided to go home only to have to have my papa Toby drive me back to the hospital since Mr.Motherfucker left my prescription drugs and after getting a refill I popped a few painkillers and took my ass to bed that night feeling useless. Since my good arm was in a cast I couldn't do much of nothing literally. I couldn't even wipe my own ass to showering yet I managed to get high using my lips but still I felt useless thinking I was going to stay like this for three months and having Mr.Motherfucker help me out made me go do a depressed stage. Sometimes I would have to repeat myself to him and because of my mom till this day I hate repeating myself and eventually we got into an argument from him snatching my panties down my leg causing it to rip to telling him what to do and what not to do and after he gave me head and a quickie the arguing stopped even though I was still mad I was satisfied physically minus the being in the cast part. Besides, that the rest of my day was cool as I ran errands having Lex go with me and after I was done we went back to my house where Scooter and Tez was there talking shit as usual and getting high yet when Mr. Motherfucker came home that night he managed to piss me off all over again by him acting slow all the damn time and since I was in a fucked up aptitude already because of the surgery and didn't take much for him to piss me off. Coming in the house at the same time we were talking about him he already knew what the drill was far as getting everyone in my house high for the night as any other night rather I had someone with me or not yet he decided to act slow as if we didn't have this convo earlier that day. Ignoring him till the budman came to my door I had Mr. Mothfucker pay for the weed at the same time Scooter was stealing out of Mr.Motherfucker book bag without telling anyone and I wasn't informed till Mr.Motherfucker brought it up and by that time Scooter had already left. Ignoring him I had Tez roll up the weed and after smoking the third blunt I went off to bed only for Mr.Motherfucker to keep talking about his stuff he stole being gone. To make the convo short I told him that he could leave since he thought I was lying when I said I didn't have it and I walked out my room to smoke a cigarette yet his ass followed me and as I sat there for a while just so he wouldn't talk to me in front of my brother I then went back in my room to go to sleep and he followed me back in my room where he told me he had nowhere else to go yet I didn't care I just needed some space and time alone since he was pissing me off. A part of me wanted him to stay but the other part of me needed for him to leave so that I can miss him and hopefully appreciate his company but before I went to sleep I had a talk with GOD explaining my situation and trying to figure out what I was going to do in general and before the convo was over I asked GOD to help me. Waking up the next day I felt the tension between Mr.Motherfucker and I yet I didn't care since he accused me of stealing his stolen merchandise. We even got into our last argument telling him if he go over his foster mom house instead of staying here then he can leave and don't come back and as I watched him pack a few of his stuff I watched him as we locked eyes for the last time and he left never coming back and after not hearing from him in two days I took it as the breakup and after writing him a note on Facebook I went home straight after my doc appointment and met Los there were we finally fucked busting both our nuts while Lex and

Tez was in the other room and when we finished I kicked his ass out and I got Tez and Lex high till I ran out of weed that Wednesday. At that time I was going through different emotions from lonely to useless to depressed yet I never showed it instead I kept myself busy from chilling with my sugar daddy getting money and weed from him so that Tez and Lex got high and I kept them high the rest of the week better yet the remainder of their visit. Anyway when Friday hit the three of us went out hitting up different spots downtown just to go back home and the early morning. That afternoon after getting a new phone since my old phone was water damaged during the time I fucked Mr.Motherfucker so I was too happy getting a new phone and afterwards I went over Mz. Trouble house this time being the single girl I always was. Going over her house I drove in Toby truck with Mek-mek, Mz Trouble and Roro driving around the east side going over Mz Trouble people house off 55th. Later RoRo left after we smoked two blunts being the only people were smoking was Roro and I things were feeling good even after he let. What I didn't know was that Mz Trouble leaving taking Mek-mek and I to her new fuck buffy house name "Baby Noodles". At first things were cool till Mz Trouble wanted me to sit in the front while she fuck Baby Noodles in Toby truck yet she never ask but also thought I was going to stay in the truck as they fucked. Leaving out the truck Mek-mek and I walked around the 116th area and after walking back to the truck we still noticed them fucking in Toby truck simply by the truck rocking back in forth letting it be known to us and the people house we were at and I was too pissed that she was inconsiderate about dragging her two friends around as if we was fucking too and after talking to Mek-mek the both of us walked back to Mz Trouble house not caring if Toby noticed us coming back without Mz. Trouble since he was watching her two kids while Mz. Trouble was getting fucked in his car. Of course Mz. Trouble was mad yet I didn't care since she was being inconsiderate that I just had surgery a week ago and even the healing process was faster than expected, I still was walking around with stitches in me plus my sling I still had on. Waking up the next day I rushed home to get dress and go over papa Toby house for a party and when I got there music was being played blunts were being rolled and the only thing I manage to drink before getting fucked up was some 1800 mix with wine and not noticing I was fucked up till I got up to stand. I even talked to Mr. Motherfucker for the second time yet the conversation wasn't about getting back together but how I treated him and truth be told he was right yet he let me treat him like that yet I didn't care. I did find out that he found a new girl at the blood bank sucking his dick in the bathroom at the blood bank then left over her house that Sunday night so I felt it was really over yet that wasn't about to stop me and my version of fun that I was doing before and after him. The next day it was my 2nd family reunion on my moms side of the family. The next day I went over Mz Trouble house planning to go over her people house on 55th yet I got a last minute call from Missty saying she wanted to go to the family reunion and I went for one reason and that was to fuck with the hoe of the family. Going there with a bottle of liquor and bud I had my cousin Baldy fake ass roll up two blunts giving him a bud to smoke and I kept it pushing. I realize it wasn't as packed as it was and this was the last time I seen my #1papa before he died. The person I wanted to come finally came and since I'm drama as Yogi and papa Toby said it started first by me seeing the hoe off the family talking and I jumping on the conversation speaking to her saying something knowing it would piss her off and just like I predicted she walked off yet slowly or surely I was following her. After talking to a few new family members and seeing some old ones I decided to fuck with the hoe of the family again this time sitting next to her at the table they were at and I sat next to her speaking while sipping on liquor in her face. I only did that knowing I would aggravate her. Interrupting the conversation they were having and let it be known that I ain't like the hoe of the family just then she got up and stood up saying "I'm tired of your shit" at the same time I took another sip of my liquor and get up with her face though face saying "what are you going to do about it, it's not like you going to whip my ass". I even went as far as making spit bobble acting like I was going to spit on her at the same time mugging her getting in her face. Of Course we were separated before the fight could jump off. Surgery and all I was willing to beat her ass at least get some hits off yet my chances were slim to none. Since one of my elderly cousins who happens to be my favorite and the same one who worked as South before they closed the school I graduated. So I had no choice but to listen to get out of respect plus if my granny was still alive she would of also hit me for starting shit. After calming down I joined the party line dancing drinking and geeking. As soon as the reunion was over we all went our separate ways but not before riding past the hoe of the family in a truck my cousin was driving and threw a plastic fork at the hoe of the family pulling off. Going home I told Tez about the altercation between me and our cousin. That whole week I chilled at home getting Tez Lex and I high off the weed and money I got from the different guys who came in my house only thing different was I had Tez with me and since he's my older brother people tend to have a problem getting pussy from a girl who has older brothers especially if they're here with them little did they know I was using them technically rather they got something out of it or not. That whole week in a half was cool yet the second almost third week of them September I had enough of Tez and Lex ways. It went from Lex thinking she had the authority to sit in my chair with her panties as if this was her house and her shit to after staying up till 5a.m or later in my house watching my t.v. to using my cabal with my light bill yet had the nerve to ask me to turn the t.v down or off. What pissed met of is my light bill getting sky high and no-one was paying but me. Better yet how about the nights they kept me up watching t.v. causing me not to sleep easily since I can't sleep while people are walking around my house let alone in my house yet I didn't complain about nothing since he let me do as I pleased so I did what I did to get us high. Truth be told there a lot of dumb niggas out her just like us females. As soon as the third week hit I was damn near fed up and pissed then there was Lex again with her mouth and to make matters worse mom was behind the starting shit going back telling Tez how I was feeling yet not defying it how I said it and Tez believed telling his gf and started the second to last strike before I reached the limit and it didn't take them long to reach that limit. That whole week I kept myself busy going from Lisha house to Meka fam spot to Mz. Trouble house getting drunk. Ever since my STNA lady told me my stress was high I decided to kick it being out the house giving them space in my house. One day I was pissed after coming home to a toilet full of shit no body but Tez did then to add insult to injury I noticed my dishes being washed with the same sponge I clean my toilet with which pissed me off it started an argument before I left my house again going back over Meka people house since Meka was up here for her own reasons. I even went to prayer yet I was told about myself and how I was being mean by the way I treated people and I felt like I disappointed GOD which is a feeling you don't want to feel. That night I decided something had to change if not for me for GOD I will. That Sunday though everything changed. Since I spent my days out I went to others house this time going over Midnight house watching the game drinking, smoking and afterwards I went back home thinking my night was going to end good yet it was the total opposite. Since I was drunk I decided to have Tez fix me some chicken in the meantime I took one of Lex brownie eating it. Thinking it wasn't a problem since both of them ate my food nor asked I ate her brownie only for her to start shit. For starters Lex grabbed my ice cream sandwich attempting to eat it yet I grabbed it smashing it in her hand and just as fast I was at Lex face Tez was in the middle of us yet we still was arguing. I went as far as getting on my knees begging to fight her. Separating us Lex started complain crying to Tez about how she felt and walking out having Tez turning 0 to 100 and after the words he said only one line I want forget. The nigga had the nerve to do the same shit my dad did 2x before calling me a handicap bitch before he walked out looking for Lex and as soon as he was out the door I locked my door and threw their stuff out my window. Afterwards I called my mom telling her Tez was coming over there and to enforce it I called the police knowing Tez would leave knowing he had a warrant leaving Lex out here by herself since she had no way back in town yet after the police came two hours later he stayed and ended up going to jail that night and Lex moved to J.B house. That Wednesday since my house was now empty I kicked it starters inviting a friend of the fam K-Mack who I used for liquor and weed to fuck, then went over Rae house with Meka to chill with guys drinking and smoking till that Wednesday when I went to Tez court date and he was released later that night and I went to bed that whole day. When that Friday came about I got drunk with Lisha and her boyfriend Kash but not before running into Mr. Motherfucker and after a convo it was planned to meet him at my house and after I got drunk I went home late meeting Mr. Motherfucker and we went to bed together as he held me. The next day I went with papa Toby to Kent Ohio with my sister E-boo and watched a volleyball game that my cousin won at the same time I got a phone call from Tink saying my mom kicked her out the house having her walk the streets of kinsman alone. Thanks to GOD I had Mz. Trouble pick her up and take Tink to her house where she was setting up for Chi-chi 5th b day party where she turned up dancing on Toby truck with her little cousin Shay-shay telling papa Toby to turn down for what and she really showed her as but the little girl had fun for her b-day. Going home that night I had Tez to talk to Tink while Mr. Motherfucker and I got drunk and high off his money and going to bed. The next day as Mr. Motherfucker left and I sent Tink with Tez while I went over papa Toby house getting drunk and when I got home I got Tink and after talking to Mr. Motherfucker I knew he wasn't coming back after he ran into the girl who sucked his dick and seduced him to go over her house instead so I took it as we not nor never fucking with each other again. Having other things to do I took Tink to the Social worker building on 40th in Euclid where after a convo with a social worker Tink was sent back home while I went home meeting a friend name J'Mar who I let hit after trying for almost two years now in exchange for money I used for weed. Other days I spent going over lil mace house chilling Meka this time meeting up with Keke and they went to Walmart while I prayed a deep convo with GOD about how I felt and apologizing for actions. Afterwards I felt better talking to him getting stuff off my chest same time I thought about my life and was trying to accept my status as a street person learning from her mistakes yet I felt anger being in the world full of fake I once called family. I had parents that didn't act like they gave a fuck about me but more like what I can do for them and how I always wanted the love from both parents yet never got it. I felt the times I needed family from the time I was homeless to clothes less no one helped nor may sure I was ok so I felt like fuck both sides my family. To this day the distance is too real and I made sure to only see family during parties and was cool with that as long as I was under the influence was cool. After all GOD was the only one who had my back minus papa Toby being transportation and letting me borrow 20$ to my dad rolling up my blunts just so he can get high. When they came from Wal-Mart we drank margaritas and called it a night. Going that Wednesday I received a letter from CMHA and, after reading it I set date to check out the apartments on 55th viewing it October 23rd. Till then I was cooling going Meka to hookah bar 2x meeting few people going to martini 6 for the first time and since it was my granny b-day I was making sure to turn the fuck up not caring how drunk I was about to get. Of Course the following day was a recovery day as I went to sleep at Lisha house going home later that night to shocking news of a guy getting murdered in the alley behind my house and even though the story was sad I was glad I wasn't there to witness it like Tez did and later they put it on the first 48. As next week rolled around I seen the viewing of the apartment that Thursday and after the viewing I linked up with papa Toby to use the money I was using to pay rent and took it to put down the security deposit while the prorated my rent for the month of October and on October 25th I had the keys to that house still having the old keys to my house slowly letting another slum landlord know I was moving soon. That Friday after getting my keys a bitch went out with Meka, Mek-mek and Mz. Trouble hitting up Martini 6 and the bar was rocking yet the only funny thing was when the security guard pointed out to Mz Trouble and Mek-mek that Meka tampon was showing exposing her string under the short dress she were. Telling her about it she act like she didn't know what I was talking about so I left the topic alone and danced the night away. Planning to go out the next day my vibe went from happy to mad less than five seconds apart thanks to my papa Toby spending the rest of the money for who knows what knowing I was using that money to move paying the U-Haul truck and buying cleaning stuff for my house. Pissed the fuck off I decided not to go out yet Meka talked me into it and that night was different then the last. For starters Mz. Trouble was putting on a show dancing on the pole exposing her pussy since she had a no pantie team developing as she went around the pole and as she was dancing money was being thrown after and slowly but surely she started a money raining section real shit and guess who was after her shaking her ass making her quick 126$ ......bitch u guessed it right) my slutty as (what people say I am) danced on that pile and after I was done I realized one of the bills was 100$ bill and I was too happy I went in the bathroom telling Meka and thanking GOD at the same time that I had enough for the moving truck and I was cool with that. Afterwards I was ready to go home and as soon as Mz. Trouble and Mek-mek got dropped off I went to Meka's people house. What pissed me off was when I asked Meka to let me out the driveway so I can get out on my side and not climb to her side yet she ignored my request and parked in the back anyway. Just so happen as I climbed to her side I seen100$ bill after looking in her front seat pocket thing for I don't know what reason honestly and picked up the1$ bill I seen Meka dropped getting out the car and I went upstairs and went to bed just to wake up early as hell for her to drop me off at the bus stop suffering a hangover earlier that Sunday morning. Anyway I had Lisha pick me up meeting new at University Circle and I got a half an oz. and was going to have Lisha rent the U-Haul while kash and Tez was supposed to help me move so I bought a thing of long island ice tea and Kash Lisha and I drank and smoked till I went to bed. Waking up the next morning I went with Lisha to get the truck and have Kash drive me to Wal-Mart to get storage containers for my clothes then to my house where Tez was supposed to help me yet he didn't because I won't give him the money till after I moved and having Lex whisper in his ear he watched as both J.B and Kash move my bed and couch while I moved my two tables and my dishes, clothes, and other little things leaving some there and going back to my new house now having papa Toby and my cousin Neal and both Neal and Kash and I moved my stuff to my apartment on the15th floor and afterwards I unpacked my stuff and soon as Lisha came to pick me up I went over her house to watch the TLC movie getting high and I went home that night sleeping at my new house waking up 7a.m the next day as I was asked to watch Meka baby and I did as I did the last few times not asking for no money yet this time lil mace mom was upset I was there by myself and sent Meka a text that she had to make other living arrangements which made her tear up real bad. After packing her shit and in her car we left to pick up

Rae and went to I-hop where we ate and afterwards I got high and we went back over Rae house and slept there. The next day was the first day of a downfall I was going down and I didn't even know it yet. Waking up that October31, 2013 I was planning on getting dropped off but it didn't go as planned. Leaving Rae house after Meka son vomit on Rae carpet Meka went to my new home and I realized Meka was in a fucked up position and didn't know where she was going after dropping me off and what bothered now was her son had vomit on him. After talking to her in the car and by me having a good heart GOD bless me with I let her spend a few days at my house but not till she gave her son a bath. That same time I thought about it in my head rather this was going or wasn't going to regret this decision just like when I asked myself was I going to regret leaving a party to entertain a guy that I too also regret. Anyway I let her bath her son and that first night was funny fucking with Meka. That day I met a guy and only talked to him because he had a blue Nike jacket which is my favorite color. Anyways that night he came with another friend who stayed on the14th floor and the four of us chilled that night but the next night I invited Los over since Meka wanted male company just to talk to and I wanted Los to cone over for his weed not planning to fuck him. I had him and Meka in my room while her son was in the other room sleep and as Los and I got high and since I ain't have cable in my house yet so I listen to music and being talkative seem to solve the problem. Things was cool yet there was a knock on my door which confused the fuck out of me since no one comes to my door unannounced and by me just moving mot telling a lot of people I was curious to find out who it was. Since I had company I had Meka go to the door and when she came back after being gone for a while saying the guy with the blue jacket name R.j was at the door without lettings Los know yet what fucked me up was the fact that the guy ask me for some weed to sell and since Los had some weed he sold him some and Meka and I split the money. As the first week went by I had planned for Meka to save up money from her job she just needed to stack up enough to find a house since she was now homeless and should only take two months but if it was to take three then so be it. By her being my best friend at the time and that was the role I played I would of did what I could. See I'm a person who learned to play the roles rather a best friend, sister ,daughter, and for others far as being a fake friend, girlfriend, to the different males I chilled with and by their actions gives me the roles to play when around people and yes damn near everyone that knows me is fake and phony, and was the definition of wishy washy and I tell it to people everytime without them even knowing I'm talking about them yet my acting game too strong and my seriousness is even better. Anyway while she was going through her personal marriage shit I decided to kick it since she was my kick it buddy and that week we went from eating at Fridays restaurant to chilling over Missty new house with her husband Mel and their daughter Pooh-Pooh eating dinner playing cards listening to music and me and my cousin Neisha was geeking. Since she knew me and how I liked to live far as keeping my house clean, not to disrespect me in anyway including stealing, tying to play me like I'm a soft yet thanks to my granny a bitch is far from that. Thinking things were going to be cool yet the second week was different and was going downhill real fast. For starters she left me in the house with her son while she entertain a guy one time bringing him to my house where I bought some weed from. Them to piss me off was on this particular night Meka pissed me off after leaving out the house with Mek-mek and Mz. Trouble meeting Juju in Longwood to fuck with a nigga who they said spit on them causing beef with the girls and me being ready to fight I was always ready. After getting in the truck I didn't realized I was at the wrong place at the wrong time or should I say reason. Meeting up we for decided to fuck up his car while Juju stayed in the truck as I slashed three ties, Mz. Trouble stashing the last. Then he came out thanks to someone telling him and my first thing was to leave since we fucked his car up yet as I was running I seen Mz. Trouble was about to fight so Mek-mek and I ran towards her to protect her thinking we're about to jump the guy yet Mz. Trouble threw a brick in his window and we all ran to the car. Thinking Juju was still in the front still and Mek-mek right behind her I ran to the other side of the truck yet soon as I touched Toby truck Mz. Trouble dumb ass ain't allow me to hop in the truck by not waiting for me to hop in leaving me outside as she drove off circling the block so I had no choice but to run the opposite way to meet her and to make things worse the guy started chasing me with a wooden stick getting two hits off me and on the second strike my shoulder popped back out of socket for the 6th time.by then I met back up with Mz. Trouble as she drove towards me while the guy ran and after hoping in the car I let it be known that my shoulder was dislocated and after waiting in Toby truck outside of Cece house while Mz. Trouble did who knows what and that house same time Chinny checked to see was I cool before Mz. Trouble dropped me off at the Cleveland Clinic where Mek-mek waited with me till I was seen. Meanwhile I had her call Meka so she could be my ride back. Right before I was sedated Meka was there yet after I woke up she was gone with my keys and after calling her several times I was heated and realized tonight wasn't my night. What made me mad even more is that I should of stayed at home and fuck the guy I met at the hookah bar instead I went out with Mz. Trouble doing something I had no business doing and my karma came just as fast as I slashed the tires in another words GOD dealt with me for doing something I shouldn't have done. Since I didn't have a ride home my Caresource insurance took care of that having a pandemics drop me off at home where I had to wait for I don't know how long in the hallway to get through the door and the elevator since Meka wasn't answering her phone. Then to make me madder I had to wait after the paramedics was knocking on my door to get in my house and when she finally came to the door the bitch had the nerve to come to the door topless then had to wait till she put a shirt on. I was confused on what made her so comfortable to be topless in my house if I wasn't even doing it and it's my house. Pissed to the extreme I still said nothing and that next day I went with Lisha and after picking up my meds for the pain I got high and spend the night at her house going home the next day. Only one week in November and Meka was pissing me off. For the next two weeks I was going to be busy babysitting, getting my hair done plus buy me an outfit for a wedding plus attend the wedding then babysit right after so I was going to be busy starting with babysitting my cousins for two days that 1st week plus I had to babysit on the 9th and 10th of November same time dealing with Meka and her male company who thought it was cool to be in my house walking around shirtless as if this was his shit. I felt like since this was my shit and my shit only I'm the only person allowed to walk like that and since I didn't out of respect I should be getting 2x as much yet still by her being my best friend at the time I still said nothing. Since her company who I met years before was on his third day of being here it was known that I wasn't into the 24/7 company and since I was leaving that Saturday morning on November 9th leaving her in the house as I went over papa Toby house to babysit for that day and Sunday. The plan was to get my hair done first but since there was money being involved I decided to get a little extra cash then go my hair that Monday the 11th. Realizing I left my hair and stuff I sent a text to Meka asking her to come 19 streets over and 10 streets up and hand me stuff yet when I taxed her that she texted me "for what" and that pissed me off I didn't even text her back instead after babysitting I went home to grab my stuff but the site I seen pissed me the fuck off. Going inside my door I noticed my whole house was a mess. When I say a mess I mean everything was dirty from my floor to my bathroom to every dish in the house. When I say every dish was dirty I mean that shit. All eight plates' four bowls and four cup plus my pots and pans were dirty from her cooking whatever she was cooking that day I left her in my house. Everything was dirty from the bathroom to the bed room to the kitchen and I was too pissed teas was running down my face and I wanted to punch the walls yet I knew CMHA would fine me so after talking to Mz. Trouble I left with the liquor I had from the party Man threw for Meka little brother and I left going straight to her house where I drunk the wine and but not before I cleaned my house washing every dish in the house. Afterwards I left going over Lisha house where she started on my hair. That night I told Meka about herself and after the convo she wanted to get her stuff so I let her do what she wanted and gave her different days to pick it up starting Monday. Soon as Monday came and my hair not being finished I left to go to Maple and babysit for the extra money and that night Meka was supposed to get her stuff yet she said she didn't have her car so I told her to try Wednesday if not Tuesday. Meanwhile I went back to Lisha house where she finished my kinky twist and after spending another night there I had to go back to maple to babysit that Tuesday and that day as well Meka was unavailable to get her stuff out the house even though I never kicked her or her son out. I knew our relationship was falling apart again so I figured it will get better after she left. Going home that Wednesday I waited for Meka nor she never came even after I sent her a text asking her did she still want to go to the bridal shower and wedding yet she never texted me back and I wasn't about to kiss her ass. That night instead of staying home to fuck "Kid", which is her brother, I left after getting an oz. of weed; since Missty called to tell me her sister Shaun was in town. I decided to see them and just as planned I left and went over Missty house. That night after going to I-hop I got high with my cousin Neisha while Shaun and her family left going their separate ways. That night Missty daughter pooh-pooh broke my phone by dropping it on the floor causing my screen to break. Since 2010 when I got my 1st official phone I had bad luck with switching phones every six months due to whatever reason my phone break from a fall, to falling off a ride, to having sex act. Since my phone was broke and the only numbers I knew off hand was my mom and papa Toby and the plan was to stay with Missty using her phone to get some money from papa Toby to buy an outfit for the wedding. By the time I got the money for the wedding outfit driving all day with Missty by the time I got the money the clothing stores were closed leaving me Friday to get the outfit and since I was supposed to babysit I decided not to go and babysit that day but to find an outfit and maybe go to the bridal shower. In the meantime I called for another phone to get shipped out. As I woke up November 15, 2013 that was the motherfucking kill. (Tattoo that date on me so you'll know it's real). Hoping my day was going to go as planned I left with Missty going to my house to get in the shower and get a change of clothes plus I had to get high before leaving back out. Being the hard headed person I was known to be GOD put it in my head to grab three outfits, my fish and my weed along with my purse and having my older cousin Eve being the last person shutting the door I left headed to City Trends in Warrensville to find me a wedding outfit yet the only thing I grabbed was the weed and after asking Missty did she want me to bring the fish she told me no and I kept it pushing. Spending over two hours in the store trying on a few different outfits Missty was on the phone with my mom telling Missty she had some important mail my mom had to give me and that she was waiting on me to meet her at Missty house. Rushing to go over there after my mom been blowing up Missty phone by lying saying she had some pills to take and at the time I thought she was telling the truth and since she has lupus I took it seriously. Finally getting to Missty house I was on a different approach. For starters my mom wasn't even there yet Meka was with Tink and the car which threw me way off. Still being dumb founded I went to the car and asked Tink where the important mail was yet Tink answer threw me way off even more. After asking her Tink didn't know what I was talking about and told me that when she got home Meka was at mommy house and after a while my mom had Tink drive with her to Missty house where I ran into them after being rushed there. Technically I was supposed to be in maple babysitting but since the wedding was a day away I focused on that. Getting back to reality Meka demanded me to let her get her stuff out my house right then and there and for a minute I did what I was told till my sense came in and I had Missty do a U-turn after passing 93rd in kinsman and back to Missty house I went and Meka followed. After getting out I went in the house and after leaving out to go to the store and coming back did I realize Meka was still outside in her car which made me mad. After telling her to leave or get out the car she never moved and kept her door locked not letting Tink to get out the car which pissed me off even more and as bad as I wanted to buss her windows I didn't want Tink nowhere around and after a while Meka finally left yet she came back with the police as if they were going to make me go home even after Meka lied saying she needed some medicine for her son and long story short the officers told Meka to wait till the morning to get her stuff and that she had to leave and as both Meka and the officers left I went back inside pissed off yet I didn't let that stop my night and eventually I went to bed. That night though I had one of my strange dreams yet I want forget this one. After being woken up for Niesha and her girlfriend arguing it took me almost 20 minutes to go back to sleep only this time my dream I had was real. In my dream I went back home and the first thing I was looking for was my strawberry toaster trotters that I just bought from Wal-Mart yet when I looked in my freezer it was gone and I questioned whoever was in my house in my dream where were they yet I never got a response . Pissed off I suddenly woke back up thinking it was real yet once I realized it was a dream I slowly went back to sleep to another dream. This time I had a dream being in my house and out of nowhere my house was burning down and all I did was run out my door running down the stairs. The next thing I know is I woke back up and I barely got sleep that whole night so soon as Saturday morning hit and everyone was awoke I stop trying to get some sleep and decided to blow down on Meka and the stunt she pulled thanks for my mom helping her and put Meka business out there from her being homeless to her having a STD by her husband who she was fucking afterwards to her being in an abusive relationship and afterwards I went home where Missty dropped me off. That November 16, 2013 was the end of a relationship rather it was real or not. As son and I mean as soon as I turned my knob I noticed the bag of books that was sitting by my door was gone and do to I knew how I left my house something was way off and I was soon to find out the Who,What,When and Why process. Opening my door I couldn't believe my motherfucking eyes as I looked at once furnished house now empty as house and it was made known 10 times that someone ran through my house or the word she used for when she told Cliff a year later "Ramshackle" and boy did she do a good job. Looking in my house I noticed everything was gone from all my dishes that I just washed to all my clothes and panties bras and socks to my household items, to my cleaning stuff to my furniture , a couch, two tables and t.v, to my sister E-boo stuff I had in my house to all my important paper work from my SSI# to my birth certificate to my #1papa obituary a long with the other three I had with me including three copies of Rae daughter's to my blinds to my shower curtain to by box screen and bed rails to all my shoes to my foot and hand brace to my pain meds to the thing that pissed me off....all my motherfucking food was gone and the definition of an empty home was mind and the only thing they didn't take was one of my tables and my mattress. I mean my cable cord was even gone yet someone took the time to place a dirty as chair and my house that had bed bugs all in it. Since my phone was broke I used some dude phone on the 1st floor yet what he told me before using his phone I will never forget. Before I asked him for his phone I asked random people who I didn't know did the see aa girl with a baby come in the building and after the feedback I got I paid attention to this dude who stay on the 14 floor that him and his friend seen a lady with her baby move out of here with four boys and after he told me those exact words I used his phone to call CMHA police as well as Mz. Trouble who met me down there with Mek-mek and Chinney the same time the police came and we all went upstairs. After making a police report and checking my house again I realized there was a burn mark in my tube and I thought about the dreams I had plus the gut feeling to grab three outfits and the fish pissed me off that I didn't listen. My mom always told me a hard heads will bring a sore ass and now I regret not doing what GOD told me to do and now I was stuck with the outfit I had on and the wedding outfit I just bought. If I would of listen I would of started out with 5 outfits with panties and socks yet I only had the panties that I wore that day with the outfit I had on plus the other outfit and no extra bra, panties or socks and since everything was gone I didn't even want to stay plus I had to go to the bridal shower that night and after what I just seen I needed to go. Leaving my house I went over Mz. Trouble house where I smoked my last blunt and gave Mz. Trouble 10$ to take me to the hotel of the where the bridal shower was at and that night I got drunk thinking about my life in my current situation as everyone around me was having a ball laughing getting ready for the wedding the next day. Till this day I can't forget November 16, 2013 even if I wanted to. After getting drunk I left with someone and went to my Uncle Curtis house where I watched the kids who were already sleep while uncle Curtis left with his group and that night I had another dream. This time I was over someone house watching Meka cousin Audrey clean out Meka car wiping it down starting on the inside. Just as I walked in the house I was greeted to Meka coming up the stairs behind me wearing a t-shirt with a light purple jacket with some jeans and her hair was brushed in a ponytail straight to the back. The whole time she was crying shaking her head saying she was sorry at the same time she was reaching out giving me a hug crying repeating the same words sorry and the whole time I said nothing. Waking up realizing it was a dream I checked on the kids who was still sleep and since I was still drunk I decided to masturbate 2x in Uncle Curtis bed going back to sleep. The night before I talked to San which is Man mom but Meka aunt telling her to tell Meka to meet me to get her stuff using Missty phone yet after I found out my house was broken into I tried getting through to San using Mek-mek phone her phone was going straight to voicemail and after talking to her that Sunday morning before the wedding I had her pick me up at Uncle Curtis house where we drove together to my house not letting her know that I knew my house was broken into and the first main suspect was Meka since her baby stuff was also gone and I had a gut feeling yet I played it cool seeing San reaction when I show her my house. Getting high on our way there I peeped San calling someone right before we got out the car and whoever she was talking to her response was "your welcome" before hanging up. Going inside my building I put my acting skills on as we approached my door. Since no one knew besides Mz. Trouble and Mek-mek I acted surprised when I open my door yet I paid attention to San expressions on her face. Watching her as soon as I got there her body language told me a lot. Starting with the dumb look she had when we first enter my room. She didn't have a concerned or worried look shit she never even walked around the house to see what happened. Instead her first and only words she repeated the whole time she was in my face was "who you think did it" and I never gave her an answer. As we left and had her drop me off to Lisha house the whole time San kept asking me who I think did it and what I told her was that I had another dream with the girl crying to be apologizing without letting her know I knew and as I left out San car going into Lisha building I prayed to God that he better get her before I do and will be truly sorry for what I did but not for why I did it. After explaining the story to noisy as Lisha over a blunt I then left rushing back to Mz. Trouble house to pick up the outfit for the wedding and meeting Missty at her house and we rode to the wedding which started late then had a problem with the guess thanks to my uncle wife saying everyone didn't R.S.V.P yet I specifically told uncle Curtis wife that certain people were going and after a long back in forth convo and my uncle Curtis apologizing for the confusion we all sat and ate and

that night I went to papa Toby house where I had to babysit till Wednesday at the same time I had to tell papa Toby what situation I was in and since I now had no clothes or nothing I use my last 80$ to go to Walmart where I bought two packs of panties, two pack of socks, two bras and two jogging pants with five shirts and stretch them outfits plus the outfit I had on the day before the wedding making it look like I had one week of clothes. I even spent my last foodstamps buying food at save-a-lot putting it in my house. Still waiting on my phone I got dropped off catching the bus back to Missty house where I stayed the remainder of the month there. As I stayed over Missty house I finally got my new phone after FedEx was giving me the run around till Missty husband Mel drove me to pick it up and I felt cool after I got me a new phone. I even had "Kid" come over that week of thanksgiving little did he know this visit was a little too personal yet I wasn't going to let him know about it yet to my surprise after going through his phone I noticed he didn't have his sister number in his phone nor an his recent contact list so I was assed out far as looking for her number. The plan was to set him up using "Kid" as bate to get to his sister and I knew I could do it and pull it off using sex in the picture yet he wasn't useful since he didn't have the information I wanted. After fucking him and he rolling up my weed he left me unsatisfied (not sexually) but he was useless and I knew we wasn't going to have a friendship nor any type of relationship because of his sister action.
Spending thanksgiving with Missty and my other two cousin and their kids I got drunk and stupid high as I baked some chicken as everyone else did their food of choice. As soon as black Friday hit papa Toby let me know I got my check and after meeting me downtown he took me to Conway to buy five outfits and more panties and socks from Walmart along with other household things. The same time I had Missty husband meet me at my house to deliver a queen size bed with a t.v, table and a recliner all for 150$ and after my stuff was all in the house I left back out to go to Family dollar for more household stuff and afterwards I was back at home taking a shower for the first time in a while instead of taking my hoe baths in Missty house. I wasn't as comfortable at other people houses like I would be if I was at home by myself and that first night I left going back over Missty

house for a few more days and afterwards I went back to the Westside to my old house since I now had Tez living in my old house with Lex. Somedays I went home a night after being out all day. I even went back to Cleveland Clinic for test done on my shoulder yet when I got the results I was informed that I was getting surgery again and I never told them the real reason of why my shoulder got dislocated again. Till then I was taking things slow yet I still had my fun. I went from going out again this time only Mz, Trouble and Mek-mek and I went back to Martini6 and peeking in other bars just to see how it looked to chilling at Mz. Trouble house where all Shay, Mek-mek and Mz.Trouble invited different male friends over including D.j and his friend Syru. I even brought a guy over with his group of friends thanks to Mek-mek acting like she was me having them come over and we had fun. Out of all the guys who came through the guys Shay bought was the funniest of them all. Things were cool as we did the usual and use the guys who came in the house for their weed and liquor and talked shit. The guys assumed they were getting some pussy just because they got us high and drunk yet all we did was use them and kick them out yet Shay group of niggas were funny and the main one who was the funniest was the one selling the weed. For starters the weed dude was the main one talking mad shit bout him fucking bitches to him getting money and jokes were being tossed across the room and everyone was cool and laughing even when the bud men tried to play his friends saying all his friends were broke and that he was the one who bought a bottle of Amsterdam meaning he was the one really broke. Meanwhile some chubby little dick nigga tried to spit game on me as if he had a chance. Giving him my fake name that let the other girls know I wasn't trying to fuck with him. Mek-Mek ignorant ass went as far as pouring liquor in my breast having the little dick nigga suck the liquor off my breast causing me to squirm off the couch just to get away from the guy running to the bathroom where the guy followed me trying to shove me in the bathroom saying he wanted to talk to me yet I wasn't trying to hear what he had to say and Mek-mek thought it was funny the whole time. Things weren't getting out of hand till the bud men was freestyle his little corny wraps talking about money and his dick being big yet when he showed Mz. Trouble her expression on her face told it all and Mz. Trouble came with the jokes talking about his dick being small yet since she exposed him he went from chill mode to taking everything serious as he was being in his feelings. After a few minutes of the weed man bitching Shay kicked him and his crew out having a laugh for the day and afterwards Mz trouble fuck toy Baby Noodles and his brother came buy and after a hour I left going home almost 5 a.m. clock that morning. Other than that the other company we had were cool to talk shit to especially the crew with LeBron James hair line that Mek-mek invited over after meeting him in the club. I barely stayed home throughout the day yet I came home on most nights one night inviting Black over using him for his weed yet I wasn't planning on fucking him just yet since I knew he was a person who like to talk about himself to him being a weed dude you will have to wait all day on just for some weed which pissed me off so I knew we would never work on the relationship side. I ended up breaking the house in with "Kid" and even though I didn't trust him since what his sister did what she did I decided to act like I was his friend not telling him what his sister did and truth be told I thought he was one of the four guys that was in my house yet I had no solid proof nor did I want him to know I was accusing him as well yet I needed him to trust me and when it comes to acting I knew what to do and what no to do and the mind games I played were easy. That month I kept myself busy going back in forth from Missty house to Mz. Trouble house to my old house on the west side going home all different hours of the night. This Christmas I spent it with Tez after spending christmas eve over Momma T's house and afterwards I went home where I sobered up the next day. Bringing 2014 in with Momma Ts and her family who I realized is just as fake as all four sides of my family and they too gave me the roles to play in their life. That night I had a blast getting geeked and dancing my ass off till 6 clock January 1st I went to bed. Later that day I met Mel and his crew downstairs with the three piece couch set giving him another 150$ making a total of 300$ to get my home furnished plus papa Toby wife gave me an old t.v so now I had two tables with 2 t.v's along with a recliner chair, personal couch chair with the regular size couch and the love seat plus a queen size bed I was in a better situation at least it felt like it. All I needed to do was do what every girl love to do and that was shopping starting next month. I even got another cable cord and after hooking it up to my t.v I got my time warner cable on and I was slowly feeling comfortable as things were slowly getting back on point. I guess that was GOD way of telling me to chill, he got this, and another words leaving it in his hands and as I saw that I like what I seen I thanked GOD since it was nobody but him who was getting me out the hole I was in. Not one friend nor family member on all four sides help me, checked up on me to see if I was ok didn't even have a shoulder to cry on and all that told me that you know who really there for you and who really just there for their benefit not caring what situations people had to face. Not can one person in my family say they did anything for me besides my dad rolling up my blunts to my papa Toby being transportation when he felt like doing it and minus his wife giving me a tv and a radio and used dish set I can scream all damn they no one helped me nor gave/give a fuck bout me like how I USED to give a fuck about them and my mom can only say she gave birth to a slave in her eyes. Even when a nigga asked I still ain't get no help and had that fuck it I ain't mad at them because a nigga made it thanks to her creator. The month of January I went from Missty to Tez house going back in forth. I even went to Mz. Trouble house but after the one night I stayed there her gas kept getting cut off since she couldn't put gas on in her name and since the breakup Toby took the bills out his name leaving Mz. Trouble to be in the house with no gas and since it was now winter time it was cold as hell and out of all the times Stan the man helped yet after the last time of it getting cut off I left her house taking my ass home with heat but not before Mz. Trouble almost pissing me off acting stupid as usual in front of company talking to me sideways as if I can't beat her ass like I did three times before. Instead of causing a seen like I was known for I ignored her biting my tongue and after we used Syru for his weed I left going home. Little did I know I found out after Mz. Trouble went a few days over Juju house was she informed by Baby noodles that the landlord switched locks do to nonpayment of rent for months and after finally getting the key to go to her house was it ramshackle like mines yet the only thing missing was her t.v to microwave to the entertainment system while other things were all stacked up and pushed to the front of the house as if someone was planning on coming back to reload. Bringing her back to my house we chilled for two days before she left going back over Juju house in the meantime I was getting ready for my 22nd b-day which I celebrated over Momma Ts house getting drunk off 1800 and Smirnoff and a bitch got too drunk too fast and next thing I know after sitting on the floor in the bathroom vomiting in the toilet I remember me going home sobering up the next day. Since I realized I ain't party how I wanted to I decided to throw me a party over Momma T house inviting everyone on my dad side of the family that I knew. Till then I was going to continue buying shit for my house including buying me some shoes since all my shoes and boots were gone. Two weeks after my b-day I decided to throw my party yet my day ain't go as planned. For starters my papa Toby never came and got me nor was the food I bought being cooked and after uncle Curtis did the chicken he finally picked me up a long with my cousin Niecypooh mom yet when I got there no one showed up who I invited. My uncle Dirt baby mama and the kids came by yet since I was really late to my own party she left and when I got there the only people who showed was the people who stayed in the house including my dad showing up and I had fun chilling with the small crew. That month of February I went either to my old house or momma T house, where we played cards, dance, drank and smoked. Although I was still hurt I never showed it instead I kicked it with different people. I even finally let Black hit after him giving me weed for Lex and I to smoke fucking him in the hallway of my old house yet this was going to be his last time since his ignorant ass bust his nut in me as if we were cool like that and he pissed me off. Same time Lex rolled up yet as I was going home that night I was noticed that Lex almost got robbed and since Tez was around the corner he flew down the street looking on west 38th looking for the two guys at the same time I caught the bus back over there to make sure Tez was cool and invited my cousin in-law K- Mack who I used to get all of us high and after everything was cool I left going back home. Since my cable was on I stayed in the house on some days and other days I would go home just to watch a show. I even had another party over Momma T house before the month was over and still got visits from "Kid" and my good old sugar daddy. I even met this new light skin cutie who I don't remember his name or age to save my life but I did let him hit after he bit me on one of my spots causing me to be horny as fuck. Even though it wasn't planned to fuck him after he went to one of my spots I let him eat the cake and afterwards we fucked and the boy felt good little did he know that was his first and last time he was getting some and he never got the picture till I kicked him out and even after I kicked him out he came back knocking on my door yet I ignored his ass and slowly but surely he got the picture. That same month I was going in for surgery so till then I chilled with the different people and there wasn't a day that a bitch wasn't high. I also went to old navy sale and bought five more outfits and two pair of tennis shoes from Champs and I saw that I was doing better the month of March then what I went through in November. Four months later I had three weeks of clothes and 3 pair of tennis shoes I came up with a goal to look good and flex while doing it and since I ain't have a job I didn't need to do shit but wake up, eat, shit, and sleep while others had to work just to do what I do every day. I also thought about the convocation I had with Mrs. Ann back in 2012 about me going through something but at the end of the day I will be fine in a house just big enough for me and thinking about what I been through the last two years I knew what she meant . The only thing was the friend part I was confused on. My second surgery was on March18, 2014 and unplanned on what I was going to do after the surgery I had E-boo go to the hospital with me this time having a surgeon from Cleveland Clinic where I got my favorite drugs again getting put to sleep. What felt like a minute was really hours and after 6hours past I was released after E-boo walked to get my meds and back home I went when I was there for the next two days having my dad stop by to wash my dishes and hit half of his blunt before he left to go over who knows house. That Friday though as I left with E-boo going to Momma T house not knowing she was staying I ended up catching the bus with my arm in my sleeve and I caught the redline and healthline back to my house by myself. Tez was supposed to meet me at my house after calling to tell me he was on his way yet he never called or showed that night having me being in the house by myself with my good arm in the cast still. Waking up the next day I called around trying to get some help and like any other time I truly needed someone no one never came through. First person I asked was papa Toby but he said because of his wife not wanting me there I wasn't allowed to stay even after I only needed to be there for a week. After I flipped out on papa Toby wife letting her know how I felt far as her treating me and my siblings like we're not hers as if I was going to treat her as if she was my granny who died 14years ago and I had enough of her playing favoritism with her kids vs papa Toby kids. She let Uncle Curtis and his family stay there but when I needed a place to stay it was a different story and there were plenty times papa Toby turned his back on me because of his wife and because of the act I knew what role to play with papa Toby. After all he was just my payee. Since I couldn't find no one to sit here with me and help me far as cooking and cleaning the surgeon nurse who I was on the phone with the EMS to be dispatched to my house especially after she found out that the STNA lady that was supposed to come out never came to change my dressing and after waiting for about ten minutes I was back at the Cleveland Clinic where I took a vacation being in the hospital. This is the main reason why I say I'm in the streets because I feel like I'm in the streets by myself by the people actions around me yet they oh so love me but where the fuck is the love at. From a nigga I fucked to people I call my blood no one that's living on earth as of June 2015 shows me the love I wanted nor need it yet don't feel sad and sorry for me yet understand why I'm the person I am today that's all. Truth be told and I'm a keep saying it throughout this book the only person who have my back regardless of my actions was and always will be GOD. After getting admitted in upstairs the first person who decided to visit me was papa Toby and afterwards I gave him my key to give to E-boo taking her to my house where she was to grab certain shit and clean my house bringing me clothes back so I could bath yet while I was thinking he did what I asked I found out papa Toby gave my keys to my dad leaving him in my house for two days and didn't know he had it till the day he visited me meeting Midnight up here so she can get me high the same time I met this guy who I seen before and after a brief flirtation convo I gave him my number as I went outside to smoke a blunt and afterwards I was back in my room waiting on the drugs to numb my pain. After finding out my dad was in my house I made him give me my key yet after giving my key back I noticed no one bought me clothes so I was chilling at the hospital with a gown and depends constipating myself since the side effects of the drugs made it that way I sort of liked the stay. After being there for a few days I was transfer to a nursing home out in Mayfield call Manor care and as bad as I didn't want to go there I had nowhere else to go so I had to roll with the punches yet this nursing home wasn't like the nursing home I went to back in 2012. For starts I had my own room with a comfortable bed to lay in plus I was allowed to order what I wanted to eat unlike the other nursing home where we ate whatever they cooked and didn't have a t.v plus the rooms were smaller. As I got settled in there I put on my Pandora playing my kick Franklin radio, popped the drugs and I closed my eyes as I let the day pass me by. Over the next four days I got cool with the staff and actually liked them and met a 30year old patient who had 2kids of her own and we played spades, casino and Remy letting the days pass us by. I even went to my therapy sessions where I had fun playing games and working out and truth be told I enjoyed my short stay there minus the odor whoever shitted on themselves. Besides that that nursing home was the shit and if I had a nursing home to go to when I get of age plus have the same staff I would go there for sure and a bitch was rocking her hospital gown and depends everyday yet I had had enough of not feeling independent and waiting to get picked up to get some clothes soap and other stuff my patience had worn out when papa Toby stood me up three different times I was fed up with the excuse he had came up with. Waking up that Sunday morning I grabbed my things and headed out the door yet I was stop by a staff and after talking to the manger and a few other staff members trying to convince me to stay which I should have did yet I wanted to go home, shower with my soap and where my clothes plus I needed to get high and wanted some dick and after the manager paid the taxi she let me go home where I got high and fucked the same guy I met at Cleveland Clinic who also worked there as valet and afterwards off to bed I went in my own home. The next day I did the same shit getting high and fucking Mr.Juju who I found out is JuciyJ baby father and after finding out and trying to ignore him I finally gave in letting him fuck me and that boy still felt good as I laid on my back and let him do what he does best and satisfy my insides. After being home for a few days I finally step outside after it being three weeks of surgery and took a trip to Momma T house where they were celebrating Momma T nephew Jug birthday and that day I had fun drinking and geeking till the early morning where I went home. I even invited Cliff back over who I finally let hit since the last time we fucked was in 2012 just like Mr.Juju. I even finally fucked the security guard that use to work at Micca old building but I didn't fuck him for free. As the days of April went by I celebrated Easter with Tez since he ain't have nothing to do nor did uncle Spanky pick us up like he said he would. Instead he was over my mom house cooking then to find out he was up here this whole time I was in the hospital which pissed me off. That night I went by Niecey Pooh house where we drank and took Jell-O shots and as bad as I wanted to go out I didn't only because of my shoulder so I went home where I did random shit with random people. I even had E-boo chill with Tez and after talking to my uncle Dirt about Tez situation Dirt fronted Tez a half of oz. and all he had to do was give my uncle 85$ keeping the rest of the profit and me being the first costumer I gave him the 10$ for the stick of gas he gave. Guess who didn't pay my uncle back, better yet guess who had to pay Tez money back......my dumb ass. As the end of the month came about I linked back up with Mz. Trouble and Mek-mek going to Applebee's while the both of the girls showed off their new car they got form income tax check and later on I went home that night. Catching up Mz. Troubled informed me on the new apartment she moved in which happen to be the same one Cece stayed in own by their father yet things wasn't as they seem to be. Stan-the-man had back pay on the water bill the water was cut off. Then to make things worse was that someone broke into the apartment kicking all eight doors in but not till after they started a mini fire in the back of the building. As soon as people moved out one by one Mz. Trouble was the last to leave yet she left with a bang by having Baby Noodles and his group of niggas scrap everything they can from the hot water tank to the toilet to the things in the basement. Mz.

Trouble even stole stuff of her own taking other people clothes and other items the whole time I was waiting outside watching her 2 kids as her and Mek-mek went throughout the apartment building finally leaving. That same day Mz. Trouble embarrassed herself some more by causing a seen after seeing Toby in his car with a girl at the Lee and Harvard plaza as she was coming out Little C's pizza. Outside in the rain Mz. Trouble first got out the car walking towards Toby car just to hit him and get back in the car just to park it and get back out the car edging on the fight. As her and Toby were fighting Mz. Trouble hitting Toby same time Toby slammed her to pulling on her yanking her in the plaza. The whole time I was in the car watching Chi-chi cry as lil Tony was sleep while Mek-mek and other stand byers were trying to break up the fight yet nether parties of the fight stop till someone who knew Toby personally told him to leave just in time for the police to chase him down Harvard while another one talked to Mz. Trouble getting her statement and afterwards I was finally dropped off at home. Waking up the next day as I was on the phone did I notice the same usual fire alarm going off yet I paid it no mind till I heard knocking at my door as I was on the phone talking to Mz.Pooh and to my surprise I was greeted with fire fighters who ordered me to go downstairs. Looking in the hallway I notice the door two doors away from me house was on fire and after a while of me being downstairs I snuck back upstairs and hid in my room where I ate my Chinese food and got high in my bathroom not wanting the people in my hallway to smell the weed and that day was a good day. As May was ending I chilled with my sugar daddy and he began becoming my save a hoe. Since I wasn't getting any help each month I either bought me clothes or shoes still paying rent, bills, for Lisha to do my hair plus household items and that little $721.00 a month wasn't working so the extra money I got from my sugar daddy or the random guys I slept with I used they money on weed and weed only. Same time I began to care for my sugar daddy more than just a father figure. The guy will always teach me something from sex to hustle and like a sponge in water I took it all in and fell in love of the father figure he was to his daughter it made me wish I had that with my own dad. I felt like he was the closet help I got figuring he knew my situation after telling him about the break in and each visit he made sure I was straight and each vast I never fucked him but 2x that year literally. See being in the streets u slowly realize while few fail to realize that you all you have. If you wanted something done u had to do it yourself unlike others who wait till it's done for them to take the credit and realize only you and GOD cares about the situation you're in and no one will care how GOD cares for you and is up to you to let GOD in your life like I did. No the road won't be easy but it's worth it at the end. Back to reality I kept a special eye on "kid" since Man was no longer in town due to him selling drugs with Meka dad in Kentucky. I still couldn't figure who the four boys were rather it was "kid", man, lil mace and Shaun or was it four random fuck niggas from Mountviews and the only person I didn't blame was Nitty on the strength he's fucking with Yoyo. I was convicted it wasn't him yet my mind was on that situation still. Even after chilling with the different fake crowds to the niggas I fucked including "kid" to all the kids I loved my mind was on what Meka did and how she did it. I even prayed to GOD about letting me know when her karma will come and praying I will run into her again for the past may be the past but it always catches up with you especially when u least expected. I even sat down and had a serious convocation for the 1st time with "kid" about his sister Meka and since "Kid" other sister Mz.pooh informed me that she told her brother already I decided to talk to him to see what he knew and what he wasn't telling me. This was also a convo to end a friendship we somewhat had and our sex life would finally be over. At first I was hoping he went back with his ex but his dumb ass let her get another boyfriend so I couldn't use that as an excuse so I told him the reason why to end whatever relationship we had yet after talking to him and Mz. Trouble both parties thought it was unfair to end a friendship. "Kid" felt like our relationship has nothing to do with Meka and me falling out. I felt like if anyone in my family was beefing with someone then I'm just as mad as my family member and in my eyes if my siblings beef with the same people I beef with and sine Meka and I was beyond beefing and I needed for "Kid" to be an enemy just like his sister and after explaining this to "Kid" he disagree on my proposal of me trying to end the friendship since I felt otherwise then dropped the subject once I found out where his head was at yet in the back of my mind I was waiting on the time I would end "kid" and I friendship till then I was going to be bothered with all the people who knew Meka just to get some info and slowly but surely I did. I realized the only fastest way I could get over a person and the situation was to disappear from everyone including the person and who the person talk to yet that was easier said than done. People didn't know that in the inside I was mentally fucked up already and what Meka did pissed me off more. To insult my intelligence she had the never to deny it yet explain to me how the fuck did she retrieve her items from her baby play pin to her clothes to the pink Dell laptop which had E-boo "why do fools fall in love" movie in there. The million dollar question is how in the hell is the police investigating my case where I have proof of the threat text messages that Audrey texted me thinking I didn't know it was her to never searching for my stolen property nor did they even contact a person. Another words the police never gave a fuck bout it for if they did they will realize by reading this book that this is based off a true story and the info I will reveal later on in the book should be way enough proof to see Meka and her crackhead, drug spun family in jail starting from drug and gun chargers to an open case with social services to admitting to a crime yet nothing happened yet. Out of all that the part my mom played in hurt me the most. Instead of letting me know Meka wanted her stuff that whole day would have been different. Instead she lied as if I had some mail knowing I didn't and as usual was the cause of the drama. Real stuff GOD knew how it played out and he has his ways of letting certain people know certain things but for both my mom and Meka to play dumb only pissed me off even more. I didn't even miss the clothes since I was planning on getting a new wardrobe yet I was procrastinating so Meka actions just made me shop earlier yet I just missed my dish set and my #1papa obituary that I will never get back nor a copy of it and that got to me . That same time Mz. Trouble had overstayed her welcome. Not even a week went past that I peeped Mz. Trouble and her same ways of living haven't changed since 2010. In my eyes and countless other people eyes Mz. Trouble needed to get her life together. She say it all the time but actions speak louder than words and after having two kids with no high school diploma and only having four jobs out her life and not even four but I'm a give it to her still she was in the same boat being homeless yet after all that she managed to hop from dick after dick fucking niggas for her own personal reason including fucking Baby Noodles who came clean to him having a girlfriend that he faithfully cheated on yet them two are still a couple after Mz. Trouble got an abortion from being pregnant with Baby Noodles baby. Shit the only money Mz Trouble was receiving was her child support from Toby while Toby had their baby staying with him and his dad. I literally watch her blow her money on molly sticks (which is nothing but kush and a pill rolled up in a blunt) or putting gas in her car driving around town. Yet I said nothing nor was I about to have her here while she do the same shit not caring her two daughters was without a stable home and since Toby kept Lil Tony, Chi-chi barely seen her sister. Still I never said anything to her feeling bad yet this one day she managed to piss me the fuck off after popping up at my house with Baby Noodles waiting to get high of the molly stick. Letting them get high I peeped Mz. Trouble getting up to go to the bathroom and Baby Noodles followed leaving both her kids unattended while Tez and I was getting high already. At first I was debating on how to approach the situation without letting Tez know what was up. I wasn't worried about fighting or upsetting people but was worried on how Tez will react if he heard conflict afraid he will turn into one of his five personalities. My brother really has five different people living in his head and he told me the names of all five this past Easter. What distracted me was the noise from her baby falling off my bed and at that moment I grabbed her baby putting her in the bathroom with her mom since Mz. Trouble thought it was ok to fuck in my house yet I shut that shit down and she got an aptitude real quick telling me she was getting her stuff to leave but little did she know that was music in my ears. The thing I learned was never help anyone who refuses not to help themselves and Mz.Trouble was the prime example. Besides I got the hint that a lot of people feared what Tez would do if he was mad including me the difference from me and the others was I was just like Tez and was willing to fight him killing him if I had to. See I had Tez as a secret weapon at certain times since he couldn't control his anger and would unleash his multi beast if I had to. Also realize people like Mz. Trouble would talk shit about my brother yet when she seen him she gave him his respect and all that shit I dared her to say about my brother to his face it all went out the window and it did nothing but make Tez and I laughed at her. Same day Mz. Trouble told Mek-mek that Tez stole her money which was a lie yet what pissed me off was the fact she waited till she left to say some shit but neither one confronted him about it till this day and that say it all how Tez got people feeling when he's in their presence. Not putting him on a pedal stool but Tez ain't have problems and when he did he dealt with it as fast as it came. A few days went past and Lex up and leaves going back to her hometown where Tez followed a few days later after going back in forth from my house to my mom's house. But when the nigga came back he had some news about him getting Lex pregnant the same time Mek-mek was also and I was excited I gave the baby a name closer to my granny.

Chapter7
As June rolled around Tez and I did our usual which was to stay high watching a show call Ridiculousness on MTV which had us laughing the whole episode. Till Tez left Cleveland again saying he had a job interview and as he left I was back to my usual shit popping up on people to see what was shaking or not. I chilled with Rae drinking where she told me about myself and how I treated Tev and after the convo I decided to hit Tev up on Facebook after I stopped talking to him for a while. I still chilled with Mek-mek and Mz. Trouble even though their relationship was falling apart for whatever reason I just know it was different not being the usual three yet I rolled with the punches as summer time hit. After being gone for a few days I found out that Tez never had a job lined up and was staying at a motel for three days before he had to leave and since it wasn't nowhere for him to go he was back in the streets. As we found out the situation Tez was in something like the one I was in two years ago so our cousin Ed#1 decided to pay his ticket back to Cleveland but as my mom intervene yet again as she always do it never happened and after being in a homeless shelter for another three days praying to GOD something will happen and to my freaking surprise papa Toby paid his ticket back to Cleveland something he didn't do for me yet I was glad he had a way back and the only thing I was really worried about was him working back at Cedar point till then he can enjoy his last week or so in Cleveland and off to Sandusky he goes. The whole trip back to Cleveland I talked to him putting God in all my conversations and Tez went from him surviving eating peanut butter for two days so I decided to fix him a meal that night he came back in town. See I never cooked for people other than kids yet by him being my brother and the heart GOD gave me I fried some chicken and cooked mac and cheese just in time for it to be done by the time he got here and he ate we watched the ending of a game got high and called it a night. The next week was cool as I went to my lil cousin Nana b day party where Lisha dropped whatever beef she had with me and after talking to her I was told it was more he/she say bull crap I was so tired of. I dropped the non-talking to Lisha yet little did she know I've been watching her ever since the 1st fallout in September 2011 and realize a pattern with her just like Mz. Trouble and

I decided not to deal with them or their using ways so by both their actions I chose a part to play or act as I should say and was going to play my part so good I was going to forget I was even acting. I also came to realize that Lisha only fucked with me for my money and to get her high yet I figured she was beneficial when it came to doing my kinky twist for the 40$ so as long as she kept my hair done I will allow myself to be bothered with her. Yup you'll be surprised who your real friends are and to make things sound stupid the ones who claim they were the realest people are the fakest one yet they don't think I know but trust me I may not be hipped on time but I never said I wasn't hipped. Just because I didn't say shit didn't mean I didn't know and honestly I was getting tired of the fake shit so I felt like I'll beat them at their own game and be just as fake as them. Anyway back to the story that night I spend a night having papa Toby drop me off the next day with Jaja and Nana in the car same time I called Mz. Trouble to drop off Chi-chi and the three of them chilled together in my house after we went to the park and me putting Mz. Trouble car in my name for 30days. The following day I went over Momma T house bringing the trio with me where we got high and played cards and at the last minute I was going to Cedar point with E-boo and Neal two little sisters Laya and Moe-moe having our papa Toby taking us the next morning just to go and even though I had my surgery three months ago I still rode certain rides still taking it easy as the day went by and when it closed back home I went where I realized Tez was gone with Nana money she left in my bathroom. After calling I found out he went to my mom house where he spent the night and just so happen my mom took my other three siblings to Cedar point. Coming back that night I informed Tez to reimburse the money he took out my bathroom and afterwards I told him that he had to leave since he was stealing little kids money now. That next day after getting high we went to the zoo and afterwards he went to my mom house where he spent the remainder of his days there leaving June 17 2014. That same year I realized Tez Po, Lisha, Mz. Trouble, my uncle Curtis mom and wife plus a few others I realized I wasn't fucking with them especially how Lisha and Mz. Trouble thought I would be fucking with them. As the ending of June came about I spent my days in the house getting high by myself drinking on occasions with different people from Rae to Lisha. I even did my usual 2 1/2 hour walk from my house to the flats downtown and back giving a total of 160 streets I walked daily. When July 4th came around I went with the flow undecided on what I was doing. The day before July 4th I went back over Nana house to celebrate her big brother 16 b-day party where I chilled drinking and geeking in the car yet we were interrupted thanks to some street niggas from Buckeye literally fault from the top of my cousin street to the end hitting cars and all and we watched as the fight was popping off and did nothing but be nosey till the police came and shut it down. Leaving with Mek-mek that July 4th it was a day full of surprises good and bad. First my day went by good going with Mek-mek to her dad house meeting him and his 1st son yet Mek-mek dad made it known that he liked what he see yet I was interested in his pockets and as bad as I wanted to fuck with her dad Mek-mek let it be clear that she wasn't feeling her dad hitting on me then after he asked me "do I like older guys?" I was mad I couldn't honestly answer the question and little did he know if I could I would add him to my client list not caring her dad was older then my dad. My happy blushing day went from that to a fuck it mood thanks to Yogi my supposed to be aunty in law feeling some kind of way bout me introducing Mek-mek to her mother as my papa Toby wife instead of saying my granny as if I ever did that before. Ignoring her I went in Lisha car to get high yet Yogi followed me talking shit from calling me handicap to saying she can beat my ass which she clearly can't but because she said them words from that day forward I lost respect for her and once I loose respect it's impossible to get it back. Her actions alone made me think about my whole dad side of the family and wondering where they were at when I needed them yet my conclusion was not to come around as I often wanted to just to avoid this drama again. Shit a bitch felt alone unappreciated and unwanted so I really wasn't losing nothing. After the party was over in more liquor was being poured and the weed was being inhaled I went home where I spent the next few days in the house and the only company I will have was dick when I needed it. I still did my daily walks as well playing my music. What I didn't expect but was hoping for was the return of

Meka and she came up here with Man who I knew I had to keep an eye on seeing if he was acting difference or not and since him Mz.Trouble and I chilled I had to act like nothing changed yet I didn't trust his ass no more than I can see him. What pissed me off is I see pictures on Facebook with my sister Tink and Meka kid meaning she was over their house. Not only that, she was babysitting three kids who she didn't even know. The thing I couldn't figure is why all of a sudden Meka did Tink hair when she never did it before as long as we known each other. I took it as Meka wanted to be cool and tight with my mom and little sister which made me feel some type of way lucky I didn't have to worry about anyone else in my family being cool yet I thought my mom did that for her own crazy personal reason and since Meka was enjoying it I made sure I would purposely continuing to fuck her brother "Kid", her ex-lover who she still had feelings for Cliff, her child hood friend Tev and I decided to talk to Man. I even kept in touch with Rae and Keke just because. I also got hipped to Mz.Trouble being close to Man mom and after being confused for a while that's when it all hit me Mz. Trouble was using Man for a place to stay and putting it all together I got hipped to Meka, Mz.Trouble and Man all staying in San new house on shaker Blvd while San moved back to the same house on Mountview where the roaches never left. I also was informed Meka got her car in the impound and since the car was never in her name she couldn't get it back and I was too happy that she lost something she couldn't get back yet I wasn't fully satisfied and desperately wanted GOD to punish Meka some more knowing what GOD does no man can touch. In the meantime I chilled with both Man and Mz. Trouble chilling in Mountview with Man people. I even had the nerve to keep a quick convo with San checking her body language and speaking some familiar faces in the hood I was known at but not from there. My other free time I chilled with my sugar daddy only this time I was trying to end our relationship since I knew it was going to have to end sooner or later thinking about his age and what I wanted from a guy yet he was making it hard for me not taking no for an answer yet slowly but surely it was going to an end. Other times I chilled with different male friends and things were going find as August came around. The 1st week of August was cool as I kept myself preoccupied from either chilling with Mz.Trouble and Man to seeing Mek-mek from time to time till spending a night over Tev house and literally kept myself busy and a bitch stayed high and drunk liquor on occasions with different people I chilled with from Ta'sha to Rae to the lady who stayed behind my building who I found out Joe who is Coco cousin who fault Ced who is Chi-chi father even though Coco take care of her. I even got back in contact with Los who I let come over just to roll up my usual 2oz of weed that lasted me three weeks and I finally let him hit for the 3rd time only this time he felt good and I liked it but not him. As usual as things were going good it also took a turn for the worst when I got a call on August 10, 2014 when I got an unexpected call from Tink saying my mom kicked her out again for the 2nd time and just like a mother protecting her kids I got dressed and ran out the door meeting Tink downtown in Tower City where some guy was trying to keep her company yet when I saw her I grabbed her and didn't say shit to her till we were safely in my house. Not knowing what to do I made some phone calls and after calling people the only one who called me back was Momma T and after speaking to her I came up with a plan. Since I had a doctor appointment that Monday after it I went to Momma T house where I dropped Tink off knowing I was going to be busy that week I needed Tink to stay put somewhere since I knew our mom was going to be looking for Tink in a few days and I wanted to make it seem like I really didn't know where she was at. That Tuesday I did the dumbest run around from 93rd in Quincey to downtown Cleveland to probate court where I did more running around, asking questions to see what I can do legally when it comes to getting custody of Tink since she been going through what Moochie, Cash, Spanky Scooter Tez and myself and since we all left Tink was now the one to feel my mom raft. After spending hours going back in forth from downtown to juvenile court I got a whole lot of different steps I could take yet the only major issue was getting custody of my sister yet since both parents were married and never had a custody hearing I had to put myself on their case and then pay for a motion of some sort and also pay for a lawyer to speak to the judge so that was a lot of money and a lot of waiting. Over the next few days I got in touch with her father Fry to fill him in on what was going on with Tink and let him speak to her dad the same time I got his information to write in the paper before sending it off to juvenile court. I even took a trip over Missty house where she gave me some clothes to give to Tink and the next day I went over Momma T house where I brought food and clothes for Tink and spending the whole day at Momma T house where I smoked with Nita fake ass who thought I wasn't hip to her stealing my weed at a party I was at over Momma T old house and went back home. That same day I got the call I been waiting on which was the cops calling asking me about my sisters where about. They even popped up at my house a few times even and both 4th district and CMHA police came and I welcomed them in my house to see for themselves that Tink wasn't with me even though I knew where she was at I never told a soul. Meantime I had Los come over and was giving him them back shots but not till he ate my box making me squirt by giving me oral and all I heard was the sound of him slurping my fluids follow by his dick which he made me squirt all over him and a bitch felt good relieving the stress I was feeling in the inside and of course a bitch stayed high just to get through the days. Shit Jessica even came over just to watch me fuck him and from the look on her face she loved what she seen. Next week I went from the finical aid office where I couldn't get any assistance after being thee for four hours then after I filled out a paper sending to the courts I couldn't admit the paper because her parents never had a custody hearing they will have to do it themselves which pissed me off. The last resort was to go back to social survives yet the day I was going to go I got a call from Momma T telling me to come to her house now. Thinking the police found out where she was at I rushed over there only to hear something a sister never wanted to hear. After going upstairs in Momma T room where both Tink and Momma T was at I listened as Tink told me my little brother Man-man friend D'nel that he was being too friendly towards my sister. As I listen to the details I found out as Tink was sleeping on the couch my brother friend laid there with her getting a free fill yet he wasn't satisfied so he eased her leggings down feeling on her ass and then attempted to stick his dick in her yet Tink woke up and as soon as he realized she was awoke he hopped up running out the front door. Another words he tried to do the side way fuck so many niggas older then him did the same thing to other female. The shit even happened to me since Vicky brother thought I was sleep with his trying to be sneaky ass. I was hurt that it would have happen to my sister and was mad it went down at MommaT house where I trusted her that Tink would have been safe. What also pissed me off was the simple fact that three people in that house had a history of being raped by close members of the family and all I could think about was thinking what if Tink would have been the fourth to get raped. I knew after this info I had to tell Tez I just didn't know when and was even scared how he would react to the situation and I was fearing that bad. I was confused how that much even happen to Tink in a house full of people. After being there the whole day with Tink I had to leave her again over there and the next day I went to social services building again and after talking to the same lady I had a plan to do a staff meeting not just yet though and after going home I met more police officers. That Friday morning I got a call from Missty telling me Tink was on channel8 news under missing person report using the picture I took at my #1papa funeral the year before. Finding out who reported her as a missing person I found out her father called the news station which pissed me off since people will be looking for her now thinking she's really missing. That night I had Lisha drop Tink off at my house where she stayed with me for two days meeting Los for the 1st time which I didn't want him to meet no one. That Monday I took her down to the social worker where she talked to the same social worker who wasn't doing her job the first few times and after the staffing meeting she was released back to our mom custody. That afternoon I called up Los, got under the influence and fucked the anger out of me...some but not all. As I did my usual keeping myself occupied I decided to let Man spend the night at my house and put him through one of my test I put people in mainly the niggas I fucked from "kid" to Tev and everyone in between and he past some of them. Anyway I left with him to go over his house on Mountview to buy my usual oz. but as I got it and plan to leave I ran into Mz Trouble and Boi-boi before I left and after not talking to Mz Trouble since she took Meka to church as if she never break into my house yet this visit she had something to tell me that I been waiting to hear. From what they had to tell me they couldn't tell me there so after driving with them to get Chi-chi from school they drove to my house where they told me what they heard. See no one believed me that Meka stole my stuff yet when I mentioned the pink Dell laptop with E-boo DVD inside Boi-Boi was curious how I knew about the pink laptop he just seen at Man house and till this day she got her pink laptop that was once in my house the and instead of leaving after retrieving her items she had other agendas. Shit someone other than GOD explain to me if she never broke in my house how the fuck did she get her pink laptop that was at my house the day before my house was broken in. Anyway after a conversation between Lil mace babymother and Meka shit hit the fans. It was said from Meka mouth "that after the conversation we last had her, San, and Audrey along with "the four guys" drove to my house that Saturday morning November 16 and some random person let them in the building. Because my door was shut and not looked like I thought it was they let their selves in taking all Meka stuff packing it in her car. Instead of leaving she had other agendas throwing my clothes and under clothes away to San burning all my papers and obituary in my fucking tub and that explained the burn mark in my tub and that strange dream I had. Then to make it worse she began knocking on random people door giving away my stuff to people in the building selling shit from my couch to my t.v. to my table and after that she had the nerve to leave my door open letting people come in my house and take all my food to my cleaning products to my box screen to all my fucking blinds and shoes then had the nerve to take my pills to sell them as well before leaving my house. Yet what put the icing on the cake was the fact that she admitted it and to me I felt like she was laughing in my face as if she would ever have the balls to admit the shit in my face. On the other hand there was a bad time for her. Fucking with a guy she already lost her car but because of her and Man getting into fights a lot San lost her section8 house forcing Man to move back with his mom and Meka moving to her brother grandma house with her child along with having to go to the food bank to the blood bank for extra foods and money since she didn't have a job yet I wasn't completely satisfied. Same time Lil mace went to jail for drugs all at the same time. After Boi-boi and Mz Trouble told me what they had to say they left and the next day I went over Lisha house filling her in on what I was told over a drink of green apple Smirnoff. Next thing on my mind was to talk to Rae to see what she knew then talk to Yoyo though see if Nitty knew something as well. I honestly still wanted Meka to suffer yet the new transformation I was turning into wanted to put it and leave it in GOD'S hand but at that very moment I felt like Meka and I was at war and even though I was mentally fucked up me and my competitive spirit was going to fight till the end. Shit I even wanted to fuck her whole family over by doing what Shorty did back in 2012 and set her family up so they can do time for selling and having drugs in the house. I even wanted to call 696 kids on San crackhead ass since she still on that Pcp shit plus drugs being around the kids is a danger in social service. Even after that I still wanted to press charges on Meka for admitting to stealing my stuff and breaking and entering my house and make her miss out on her son growing up Cookie style off the show Empire. Then after all that I will feel satisfy real shit. Even though I was pissed I managed not to show it but express it by kicking it my way from sex to getting drunk partying. True enough Tev was my boyfriend after coming over September 38th asking did I want to do the relationship thing after I fucked Los that morning and fucking Tev that night and even though I was now in a relationship I still fucked around starting with his friend "kid" to his friend Cliff, to Dj to Mar to Mr. Juju and I didn't fuck them all in a week yet throughout the week I will chill with three to four guys a week let alone during the day and still had time for Tev. I went from using guys to take me places to rolling my blunts to having someone to talk to which was "Kid" or J'Mar and Tev was just there to be there. One time Tev and D.j met thanks to D.j popping at my house yet Tev didn't know I fucked D.j before and thanks to E-boo being there it was possible to pull it off. I actually used E-boo a lot through the day's she was here having Dj meet "kid" to Tev, to having Los meet people from J'Mar who I only fucked three times to D.j not caring that some were hip to the fact that I have a selection of guys to fuck. Boi-boi even witness a whole day of me in action while he was with Mz. Trouble seeing Cliff come then Tev then J'Mar and I only let Cliff and

J'Mar hit not even fucking Tev that day. See ever since sweetest day Tev piss me off after not hearing from him till the day of sweetest day and instead of fucking him I linked up with Mr. Juju and that same night Tev got in a car accident so the girlfriend role I played I went to his house and to surprise I was in his room and found a use condom on floor next to the trash can and a wrapper to a magnum condom by his bed. Even after asking him about it he came with a lame excuse saying his little brother used his room to fuck his girlfriend yet did Tev forget that he told me years ago that he was the only child on his mom side and didn't know all his siblings on his dad side who also stayed out of town. I realized he too was playing the game he never realize I've been playing since day one. I wasn't even mad as I wanted to be mad only cause I was doing me from the very get yet I felt betrayed and thought it was funny so I was going to make a laugh out of it. For starters I barely seen him and fuck him and since he never complained I wasn't stopping. shit out of all the guys who came in and out throughout the day, they gave me more attention than Tev and I realized it was a problem and only time will tell till we broke up again. I also cut off my sugar daddy since he spent me on his payday and instead of telling me he couldn't come give me the money I wanted he never called and I never called and I put him on the block list. If I wasn't with my male friends since I don't even have a handful of female friends I went over Momma T's house where I played cards, drink, talk shit and listen to music and other days I stayed at home getting high by myself watching cable or listening to music having a drama free productive time being alone. I still did my little investigation regarding what Meka did and do to my body reaction acting a different way then my mind my thoughts were different real shit. If the bitch just will let me fight her maybe it wouldn't be no more beef not saying we were going to be besties again but the grudge will be gone once and for all until then I'm going to always feel a certain type of way till I get justice as the United states put it. Asking around I found out she told more people about what she did including her ex lover Cliff who I was fucking and the word he said that she used was "ramshackle" which pissed me off. I did feel a little sad for the shit she had to go through yet the difference from me and her was that she had family to help her in the time of need where I on the other hand was out for myself by myself so in my eyes she was cool. I still wanted her to pay more yet the only main reason why I didn't do nothing physical was because of GOD but I can't say if I was to see Meka I won't fight her since my body might react different to my mind. I even went to see Man and told him what Cliff told me just for his response and body language. it did let me know "whatever was between Meka and I was between her and I" yet he didn't deny that she broke into my house but I still couldn't tell rather Man had something to do with it or not but I did feel like he gave me permission to do what I got to do. Since me and Man relationship was based on friendship and because of how he said what he said as well as Boi-boi for the information I decided other then Man, Boi-boi and Nitty other than that everyone else from Mountview was a suspect even I know half of them niggas ain't had shit to do with it I believe they all knew yet I knew niggas was talking and word of mouth is key yet don't believe everything what people tell you yet take it in consideration. The other part of me was trying to do the forgiveness because I need GOD to forgive me for my sins. The problem was actually meaning it and I had to forget yet it was easier said than done. I still wanted her to hurt physically far as leaving an imprint or permanent thing that she will forever remember and the only reason why I wanted or felt like that was because I wanted her to go through some shit just like I did since I was more emotionally hurt. See the thing was for her to always remember what she did to me having the regretful feeling and that's a feeling I wanted her to feel her whole life till she die and from the shit I witness in life I knew that's a feeling you don't want to die feeling. Anyway my days were cool as the emotional as holidays came around I decided get drunk whoever I was going to spend time with during the holidays since I don't go over my mom house nor went over no family on my mom's side and didn't want to intrigue on my dads side of the family, especially without an invite and since everyone around me had they on levels of loyalty (let them say it) I really don't like to be bother and was with friends and their family yet this Thanksgiving wasn't what was expected. This Thanksgiving was supposed to be spent over Mz. Trouble sister Cece house getting drunk, eat unhealthy food and the next day was a recovery day yet as the day went by plans were changed and we all went over her dad house Stan the man house along with his two sons and his babymama. Since I was already drinking before I left the house and soon as I got there we all ate and after I was done eating I headed towards outside to smoke since I couldn't smoke in his house. Meeting Stan the man at the door, he opens it for me as I bend down in front of him grabbing my boots. I only did it so he can have a view of my ass since I had on a pair of leggings yet as I got my boots he told me to do it again and watch what happen and like as a child doing their parents duties I did it again curious of what he had in mind and I was soon to find out. He went from feeling on my pussy to me giving a taste of my tongue by giving him a quick blow job while his babymama and the rest of the family were upstairs. I thought the thing was funny since his babymama was right upstairs and another reason I did it was the fact that Mz. Trouble thought I couldn't fuck her dad but ever since the visit when he came over to my house back in 2011 where I open the door wearing my bra and shorts. Since then I been talking shit to Stan the Man and telling Mz. Trouble know that I can fuck her dad yet she never believe me yet when the opportunity presented itself I knew I could fuck him for sure. The thing that I like about him was the father figured, independent he played and I fell in love with that shit mainly because I liked the authority of a man that I lacked thanks to my dad not being around as I was growing up and when I say around I mean having an effect on my life instead of screaming "I'm your father". After I stopped and stepped outside to get high I went back in the house where the flirting game began between Stan and I and knowing that I could fuck him I decided to tease him by taking off my panties and only Stan the man got the picture. Afterwards the night became too personal for me and I was dropped off after where I spent Friday sobering up. That night going to bed I had a convo with Tev asking can I give him 20$ for a Wi-Fi bill (so he say) as if I don't know he need it for gas, as if I'm a give him or (let him borrow) some money knowing he got two jobs staying with his mom to top it off I already let him borrow 10$ on my food stamps card back in 2012 and because of that I stole my 10$ back from him after a visit to his house. Anyway I then had enough with him and his stupid lies I decided to piss him off after he made a big deal about not spending time with me for the holiday yet he had enough time to pick up some money that told me the nigga must not know me really. So instead of arguing with him he had the nerve to hang up on me then after calling him back he didn't want to talk so I hung up. The next day he had the nerve to see if he was going to still get the 20$ and I acted just as dumb having him think he was getting the money having him waste gas coming to my house knowing I knew he needed it for gas. Just as planned that started the argument and the break up and I did the same shit before him, during him, and after him. After that incident I decided to get a new phone and new number plus switch phone companies. I don't want a lot of people having my number including my mom, Tez since he never reimburse now owing me 150$, and a few niggas from, my sugar daddy to Tev and that three days after the break up did my papa Toby ordered me a new phone .That week I fucked Mr.Juju for the last time since I was cutting his cheating ass off since I knew he still was cheating on Juicy j yet I can't lie his dick was on fleek so I know why she stayed but he got to offer more than good dick to stay with a nigga let alone a nigga that cheats. That weekend though was the usual unexpected weekend starting with Chi-chi writing a letter to her mom starting how she felt about not going to school all week saying "I miss three days of school, not one but three " and that alone was too funny yet sad as fuck as Lisha and I listen to the words thinking how this 6 year old can say and feel. Amway I spent that weekend with Mz. Trouble that Saturday since my phone was off and I was still waiting on my new phone in the mail. Mz. Trouble came over and we chilled finding out she been staying with Boi-boi mom since she was still homeless. That Sunday we went to Coco house for a minute planning on going to my house to get dropped off yet as soon as she pulled out the driveway her tire had a flat as we were going down the hill. I was too pissed and what was I going to do besides catching the bus home. I knew papa Toby was going to be there Monday dropping my phone off so I needed to get home yet I don't know how was I. Since she wasn't far from her dad house and neither of us had a phone we decided to go to his house since he's a mechanic. As we went there I was planning on leaving after he fixed the tire thinking he was going to put a donut on there yet after we went upstairs he came back with sheets throwing them at us which confused the fuck out of me. Asking Mz. Trouble to have her dad explain to us what was going on this nigga said we had to spend the night because he was going to fix it in the morning and I was pissed. For one I wanted my new phone and second I didn't like spending a night over people house especially a parent yet in the back of my head I knew what was soon to come. Asking Mz. Trouble to stay up with me she didn't even last an hour then Chi-chi decided to fall asleep right after leaving me up by myself.....will I thought I was the only one up till I head Stan the men calling my name and after ignoring him for a while I followed him in the bathroom where I bent over the sink as he gave me his stroke. After a while he stopped getting paranoid Mz. Trouble was up. After he checked the house he realized everyone else was still sleep and wet proceed in his son Boogie bed room where Stan the men spread me across his son bed climbing on top of me diving in till we both bust out nuts and after washing pussy I slowly fell just to wake up three hours later to his son Boogie getting ready for school and him and Chi-chi being up I stayed up as I waited for Stan the men to fix the tire finally leaving that afternoon just in time for me to miss papa Toby yet he left a note letting me know he had my new phone and new number. That night I went over Mz. Trouble cuzzo house drinking and that night I stayed home till 12 pm Dec 9th getting my new phone and the first thing I did after fucking a friend for a half and three loud blunts yet he only hit for a few minutes in his truck and after picking up her cousin I hit up tattoo Tom and got Walking Testimony across my back and adding foot prints two days later. The next week I chilled with Mz. Trouble not letting her know I fucked her dad. I even took a trip to Rae house to drink with her and her boyfriend on two occasions. In my head I like to chill at the end of each year and honestly ever since my granny died I disliked holiday's and that holiday spirit went out the door so each and every holiday I use that as an excuse to get drunk and smoke until it was all over. That Christmas I was going to stay home and drink, watch since movies and eat yet Mek-mek and I went to the movies to see the "Gambler" starring Mark Walbuger me getting drunk and after I went to Momma T's house to see her family who act more like my family then my actual family with they fake asses and after getting a plate I caught a ride with papa Toby and went home recovering the next day. That 28th of December I did my last fucking for money for money weed (hopefully) and decided to slowly cut off niggas in my contacts. Like I still wanted to fuck but some I just didn't want to fuck the same people I been fucking and wanted something new real fast. Besides slowly but surely Jessica started fucking the same niggas I was fucking and let's just say she's still doing that but the only nigga she didn't fuck was Tev yet she sucked "kid" dick while I watched yet I told him not to fuck her again. Others I just wanted to move on as if the fire "was still there as if it was any good". That December 31st I started my new years early chilling with Rae and her friends Mook drinking Grey Goose and afterwards I left with them on our way to her boyfriend house getting dropped off at the rapids and having Rae boyfriend mom pick us up. Slowly the party began since we were the first people there and afterwards more people came while drinks were being drunk and weed was getting smoked and it was cool planning on bringing 2015 in with the new faces yet my sister E-boo called and wanted me to come over and since she stayed down the street from where I was at I took that 20 minutes walking to Momma T's house where I drank and smoked some more and spades were being played not paying attention to the time till E-boo warned us having five seconds left. There I was at that moment 5, 4,3,2,1 happy New year's and boom it's 2015 and I made it this far about to be 23 and went from nothing to getting it all back 2x thanks to GOD who never took his eyes off me since I was conceived in my mom uterus. Yet I learned valuable lessons I'm hoping the person who reads this will as well. It's not just about how my life was or a life of a disable kid but about a story letting others know who's in a bad situation that we all have one and the path we took was made for us. I'm just a regular girl living life that's trying to figures out her purpose yet she thinks she knows it having a clue on which is letting people know that everyone has a story and even though (I) feel alone we're not alone. The thing you have to realize is to never give up and I learned as long as I got king Jesus, I don't need nobody else(in other words) as long as I got GOD on my side no one and I mean no one can sit me down and stay down. The road may not be easy but it's fit for you and you only and it's worth it at the end. Look at Michael Myers and Jason or read about the bullies and what they turn other people to do then understand why they are the way they are. Another thing people have to realize and I'm a prime example of why you should never judge a book (figure) by its looks or what it seem as because everyone and I do mean everyone have another side to things rather we let go of our past or let the pass control us just know it's ok to be nice to others for you never know what they're going through and may need a shoulder to cry on. I wonder why Tez was the way he is yet I now understand why he is the way he is only because the past makes us who we are today so the next time someone ask me why I am the way I am or why I got the mean look on my face my simple reply is read my book and see if you can do what I do how I did it and walk away.

To be continued............

Made in the USA
Monee, IL
18 February 2020

21959112R00085